Critical Reasoning

All the virtues of the first edition – lucidity, judicious choice of realistic examples, emphasis on techniques rather than learning lists of fallacies – are retained in the second edition. The changes are unobtrusive and for the better. The updated examples maintain the topical and contemporary feel and serve to underline the practical importance of the techniques that the book propagates.

John Divers, Leeds University

We find in *Critical Reasoning* discussions of the analysis and evaluation of reasoning, and of recognising implication. Then there is a chapter on clarity and precision, and summarizing arguments, and a final chapter on the evaluation of extended arguments. All of this is done with admirable clarity, and supported by a wealth of useful examples and exercises.

Philosophical Books

We all engage in the process of reasoning, but we don't always pay attention to whether we are doing it well. This book offers the opportunity to practise reasoning in a clear-headed and critical way, with the aims of developing an awareness of the importance of reasoning well and of improving the reader's skill in analysing and evaluating arguments.

In this second edition of the highly successful *Critical Reasoning: A Practical Introduction*, Anne Thomson has updated and revised the book to include new and topical examples which will guide students through the processes of critical reasoning in a clear and engaging way. By the end of the book students should be able to:

- identify flaws in arguments;
- analyse the reasoning in newspaper articles, books and speeches;
- approach any topic with the ability to reason clearly and think critically.

Anne Thomson is Honorary Lecturer and Fellow of the School of Economic and Social Studies at the University of East Anglia.

Critical
Reasoning

A Practical Introduction

2nd edition

Anne Thomson

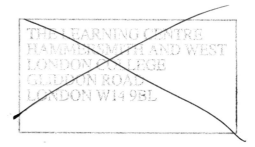

Routledge
Taylor & Francis Group

LONDON AND NEW YORK

First published 2002
by Routledge
11 New Fetter Lane, London EC4P 4EE

Simultaneously published in the USA and Canada
by Routledge
29 West 35th Street, New York, NY 10001

Reprinted 2003 (three times), 2004

Routledge is an imprint of the Taylor & Francis Group

Typeset in Sabon and Bell Gothic by
Florence Production Ltd, Stoodleigh, Devon

Printed and bound in Great Britain by
TJ International, Padstow, Cornwall

British Library Cataloguing in Publication Data
A catalogue record for this book is available from the British Library

Library of Congress Cataloging-in-Publication Data
Thomson, Anne.
    Critical reasoning: a practical introduction /
Anne Thomson – 2nd edn
    p. cm.
Includes bibliographical references and index.
1. Critical thinking. 2. Reasoning. I. Title.
B809.2.T48 2001
160–dc21   2001034880

ISBN 0–415–24119–7 (hbk)
ISBN 0–415–24120–0 (pbk)

Contents

Acknowledgements

Law School Admission Test questions are used with the permission of Law School Admission Council, Inc., Newtown, Pennsylvania, USA. These questions appeared on LSAT forms during the period 1981 to 1986.

I am grateful to *The Independent*/Syndication, *The Guardian*, *The Observer*, News International Syndication (© Melanie Phillips/Times Newspapers Limited, 10 September 2000), A. M. Heath and Co. (on behalf of Janet Daley), Thomas Barlow, Professor Richard Dawkins, Anthony Grayling and Jeffrey Miron, P. A. J. Waddington and *Police Review* for granting me permission to use articles which have been published in newspapers or journals. While reasonable effort has been put into obtaining permissions prior to publication, there are some cases where it has been impossible to trace the copyright holders or to secure a reply. The author and the publishers apologise for any errors and omissions and, if notified, the publisher will endeavour to rectify these at the earliest possible opportunity.

Thanks are due to colleagues (or fellow 'critical thinkers') Roy van den Brink Budgen, John Butterworth, Nick Everitt, Alec Fisher and Nigel Warburton; also to Tony Bruce and Siobhan Pattinson of Routledge, who have been helpful during the preparation of this second edition.

The book is dedicated to my husband Andrew, to my sons Mark and Neil, and to their wives Erica and Tanja, for making family life such a joy.

Introduction

Sir: Martin Kelly ('Fishy business in Loch Ness', 28 March) reports Dr Ian Winfield as saying that the fish stocks in Loch Ness are not big enough to feed a monster, therefore a monster does not exist. He confuses cause and effect.

It is perfectly obvious to me that the reason why the fish stocks are low is because the monster keeps eating them.

(Peter Stanton, Letters to the Editor, *The Independent*, 31 March 1995)

Sir: I read with disbelief James Barrington's letter (31 December) in which he contrasts foxhunting and fishing. He argues that the League Against Cruel Sports does not campaign against angling, because most fish which are caught are either eaten or returned to the water. Does that mean that the League would stop campaigning against foxhunting if the victims were turned into stew afterwards?

(Patricia Belton, Letters to the Editor, *The Independent*, 4 January 1994)

This is not a book about whether the Loch Ness monster exists, nor one about whether foxhunting is more cruel than angling. What the two extracts above have in common is that they are examples of reasoning – the first one perhaps tongue-in-cheek, but reasoning nevertheless. This book is concerned with helping readers to develop their ability to understand and evaluate reasoning.

Reasoning is an everyday human activity. We all think about what we should do and why we should do it, and about whether – and for what reason – we should believe what other people tell us. We see examples of reasoning in our favourite soap operas on television: the single mother who allows the baby's father to help with child minding because this will enable her to pursue her career; the parent who concludes that his daughter must be taking drugs because this is the only plausible explanation of her behaviour; and the jurors who struggle to assess whether the abused wife killed her husband due to provocation, or in self-defence, or at a time when her responsibility for her actions was diminished.

One dictionary defines reasoning as 'the act or process of drawing conclusions from facts, evidence, etc.'. Since it is clear that we all do this, the purpose of this book is not to teach people to reason, but to remind them that they do not always pay attention to whether they are reasoning well, and to provide the opportunity to practise reasoning in a clear-headed and critical way. This kind of approach helps us to know whether the conclusions which are drawn from the facts or evidence really do follow, both when we ourselves are drawing conclusions and when we are assessing the reasoning of others. However, the use of the word 'critical' is not intended to suggest that, when we evaluate other people's reasoning, we must restrict ourselves to saying what is wrong with it. Critical evaluation involves judging both what is good and what is bad about someone's reasoning.

Reasoning well is a skill which is valuable to anyone who wants to understand and deal with the natural and social worlds. Scientists need to reason well in order to understand the causes of phenomena. Politicians need to reason well in order to be able to adopt the right policies. But we cannot leave reasoning to scientists and politicians, because we all want to know whether what they tell us and what they prescribe for us is right. So reasoning well is an important skill for all of us.

Critical reasoning is centrally concerned with giving reasons for one's beliefs and actions, analysing and evaluating one's own and other people's reasoning, devising and constructing better reasoning. Common to these activities are certain distinct skills, for example, recognising reasons and conclusions, recognising unstated assumptions, drawing conclusions, appraising evidence and evaluating statements, judging whether conclusions are warranted; and underlying all of these skills is the ability to use language with clarity and discrimination.

In common with other skills, reasoning skills can be improved and polished with practice. If we think of critical reasoning as analogous to a game, we can see it as involving a set of particular skills and also the ability to deploy this set of skills when engaged in playing the game. In tennis, for example, players need to be good at executing particular strokes – driving, volleying, serving. But, in order to win a game, they need to be able to put these skills together in an appropriate way, and also to be able to respond to moves made by their opponent.

When 'playing the game' of reasoning, we need to be good at certain basic activities, such as drawing conclusions and evaluating evidence. But we also need to be able to put the skills together in order to present an effective piece of reasoning to someone else, and we need to be able to respond to the moves in reasoning made by others: for example, when someone presents us with a piece of evidence of which we were unaware, we need to be able to judge how it affects our argument. The tennis coach will improve the tennis players' ability by sometimes requiring them to practise particular skills and then requiring them to play a game in which they must remember to deploy those skills and also select the appropriate strategy.

This book offers the reader the opportunity to practise particular reasoning skills, and sometimes to 'play the game' of reasoning by deploying a set of skills. Each chapter focuses on particular skills, and presents short passages of reasoning on which to practise these skills. Model answers to a number of the exercises are given at the end of the book to enable readers to assess their progress. The reader's overall ability is developed by longer written passages for analysis and evaluation. As readers' command of skills improves, so their ability to analyse and evaluate the longer passages – and 'play the reasoning game' – should improve.

For the most part, these exercises offer practice in understanding, analysing and evaluating the reasoning of other people, rather than asking readers to focus on their own reasoning. There are two good reasons for this. The first is that it is necessary to illustrate the structure of reasoning, and this can only be done by presenting particular examples. The second reason is that it is often easier for us to recognise problems in others' reasoning than in our own. Improved skills in evaluating the reasoning of others, and the willingness to apply the same critical standards to your own reasoning, are important first steps towards developing the ability to produce good reasoning of your own. Moreover, some of the exercises which suggest working with a partner, as you might do in class, will begin to make you aware of the need to present good reasons for your beliefs and conclusions, and will give you practice in responding to criticisms and questions. The final exercise suggests subjects upon which you can practise the skill of devising and constructing better reasoning of your own.

It has already been pointed out that the ability to reason well is important in everyday life – in understanding, for example, the reasons upon which politicians base their policies, or the evidence presented in a court of law. It is also true that almost every subject of academic study, both at school and at university, requires an ability to reason well. However, most subjects are not taught in a way which requires students to think about their own thinking processes. Hence it is possible to become good at reasoning about, say, geography, without realising that you have developed skills which apply in other areas. The approach presented in this book does not require any specialist knowledge – the passages of reasoning are on topics of general interest, such as would be discussed in newspapers and can be understood by the general public. But it does require you to think about the nature of reasoning, so as to acquire the tendency to approach reasoning on any topic in this critical, analytic way. In other words, these reasoning skills are transferable; they will help students in their reasoning on a wide range of topics, including their own specialist area. Practice in dealing with reasoned argument will also help students in their essay writing, since in most subjects a requirement of good essay writing is that ideas should be presented in a clear, coherent and well-argued way.

The ideas underlying this text are related to the academic discipline known as Critical Thinking, as can be seen from the following quotation from Edward Glaser, co-author of a widely used test of critical thinking, the Watson–Glaser Critical Thinking Appraisal: 'Critical thinking calls for a persistent effort to examine any belief or supposed form of knowledge in the light of the evidence that supports it and the further conclusions to which it tends.' (Glaser 1941: 5). The Critical Thinking tradition, which derives from both philosophy and education, originated in the US. Some of its foremost American proponents were, or are, John Dewey, Edward Glaser, Steven Norris, Robert Ennis, Richard Paul and Michael Scriven; in Britain, the name most closely associated with Critical Thinking is that of Alec Fisher. Readers who are interested in learning more about the subject will find details of these authors' works in the bibliography at the end of this book.

It is now possible to study for an A/S level in Critical Thinking, and the skills which are assessed in this examination are very closely related to the skills which this book seeks to improve. However, the book should not be seen merely as an aid to improving one's skills for the purposes of assessment, though it will certainly function admirably in this way. Its influence will be much wider than this, enabling readers to deal effectively with reasoning in every sphere of their lives.

Chapter 1

Analysing reasoning

We cannot begin to evaluate someone's reasoning if we do not understand it, or if we understand the words but fail to grasp that reasons are being offered for accepting a point of view. The skills upon which this chapter focuses – recognising reasoning, and identifying conclusions, reasons and assumptions – are the most basic abilities; upon them the important skills involved in *evaluating* reasoning (the focus of our next chapter) depend.

Recognising reasoning and identifying conclusions

Reasoning is, of course, presented in language, but not all communications in language involve reasoning, so we need to be able to pick out those features of language which tell us that reasoning is taking place. It is clear that we use language for a variety of purposes. For example, we may use it to tell a joke, to insult someone, to report factual information, to describe a scene or a personality, to tell a story, to express our feelings, to explain why we have acted in a particular way, to ask questions, to issue orders. What most uses of language have in common is the attempt to communicate something to others.

Sometimes we want to persuade others to accept the truth of a statement, and one way of doing this is to offer them reasons or evidence in support of this statement. This is the essence of argument. The simplest examples of arguments occur when someone, who believes some statement, will present reasons which aim at persuading others to adopt this same point of view. In more complex cases, someone may wish to assess and evaluate someone else's reasoning, or someone may be reasoning about their own or someone else's reasoning. We all use language in this way, often without thinking of what we are doing as being something so grand as 'presenting an argument'. For example, someone might say:

> He must be older than he says he is. He told us he was forty-two, but he has a daughter who is at least thirty years old.

Here reasons are being offered for the conclusion that 'he must be older than he says he is'. So this simple, everyday piece of communication is an argument.

Here are some more very simple examples of argument. As you read through these examples, think about which statement the author is trying to get you to accept (that is, the conclusion), and which statements are being offered as reasons for accepting the conclusion:

> The bus is late. It must have broken down.

> That bird can't be a robin. It doesn't have a red breast.

> You should try to appear confident in your job interview. The employers are looking for someone who can speak confidently in public.

> Children learn languages much more quickly and speak them more fluently if they start to learn them at an early age. So if you want your children to be bilingual, you should speak two languages to them from the time they are born.

> She didn't turn up for their date. She obviously doesn't really want to be his girlfriend. If she'd wanted a serious relationship with him she wouldn't have missed the date.

'Argument indicator' words

The language of reasoning can be very complex, but there are some relatively simple linguistic clues which can signal that reasoning is taking place. Certain characteristic words are used to indicate that someone is presenting a conclusion, the most commonly used being 'therefore' and 'so'. For example, the argument presented in the first paragraph of this section could be written as:

He told us he was forty-two, but he has a daughter who is at least thirty years old. So, he must be older than he says he is.

'Hence' and 'thus' can also function in the same way as 'so' and 'therefore', though they are less commonly used. Other words may indicate the presence of a conclusion, for example, 'must', 'cannot'. In the original version above, the word 'must' is used to show that the reasons offered force us to draw the conclusion. The word 'cannot' could function in a similar way, since the conclusion could have been expressed as follows: 'He cannot be as young as he says he is'. Sometimes the word 'should' can signal that someone is presenting a conclusion, because arguments often make a recommendation. This is shown in two of the examples above; the third, which recommends appearing confident in a job interview, and the fourth, which recommends speaking two languages to babies. All of these 'conclusion indicator' words have other uses in addition to their function in arguments, so their presence in a written passage does not guarantee that an argument is being offered. However, they are useful indicators in assessing whether a passage contains an argument.

Recognising arguments without argument indicator words

Some passages which contain arguments have no argument indicator words. In order to recognise them as arguments, it is necessary to consider the relationships between the statements in the passage, to assess whether some of the statements can be taken to support a statement expressing a conclusion. For example, the following passage can be construed as an argument:

Knowing the dangers of smoking is not sufficient to stop people from smoking. One third of the population still smokes. Everyone must know that smoking causes lung cancer and heart disease.

This passage is clearly presenting as a statistical fact that one-third of the population smokes, and as an obvious truth that everyone must know the dangers of smoking. It is using these reasons to support the conclusion that knowing the dangers is not sufficient to stop smokers from smoking.

Note that the only candidate for a conclusion indicator – the word 'must' – appears not in the conclusion, but in one of the reasons. Yet, we can be clear that the last sentence is not the conclusion, because no appropriate evidence (for example, that there have been programmes to educate the public about the dangers) is offered. Note also that in this example, as well as in our first example, the conclusion does not appear at the end of the passage. We need to be aware that conclusions can appear anywhere within a passage, even though it is possible for us to 'tidy up' an argument by writing out the reasons first and ending with a conclusion introduced by 'so' or 'therefore'.

We have now considered two things we might look for to identify the conclusion of an argument:

1 conclusion indicator words;
2 the claim for which reasons appear to be offered.

Note that if we have identified a conclusion, we have also identified the passage as an argument, or as something which is intended to be an argument. If we have identified the conclusion by finding conclusion indicator words, then it is reasonable to regard the author as intending to present an argument. Earlier, we introduced the term 'argument' as one way in which people use language when they are attempting to persuade or convince others of the truth of something – that is to say, when they have a particular purpose. However, when trying to assess whether a written passage presents an argument, we are not solely trying to guess the purpose of the author in writing the passage. We can also attempt to interpret the way in which this piece of language functions: this is what we are doing when we identify the conclusion by the second method, that is to say by looking for the claim for which reasons appear to be offered. If a passage can be written out as a series of reasons supporting a conclusion, then it can be construed as an argument, even if the author did not quite intend it in that way.

Nevertheless, it is often useful as a first step to consider the purpose of a passage when trying to decide whether it is an argument. If you ask yourself, 'What is the main point which this passage is trying to get me to accept or believe?', you can then underline the sentence which you think expresses the main point. The next step is to check whether the rest of the passage contains a reason or series of reasons which support the main point. You do not need to worry too much at this stage about whether they give conclusive support, because you are not yet attempting to evaluate the reasoning. Consider whether they are relevant to the main point, and whether they support it, rather than counting against it. Do they provide the kind of evidence or reasoning which one would need to present in order to establish the truth of the main point? If you are satisfied on these matters, then you can take it that you have identified a conclusion of an argument, and thereby decided that the passage is an argument. You may find it useful to tidy up the argument by writing it out as a series of reasons, followed by your chosen conclusion, introduced by 'so' or 'therefore'.

Identifying conclusions

In this section are some examples in which we put these recommendations into practice.

> The new miracle drug Amotril has caused unforeseen side effects of a devastating nature. Careful testing of the drug prior to its marketing could have prevented the problems caused by these side effects. Therefore, no new drugs should be released for public consumption without a thorough study of their side effects.
>
> (Law School Admission Test, 1981)

This argument presents its conclusion in a straightforward way, and this helps to make it an easy passage to analyse. We first notice that the word 'Therefore' introduces the last sentence, so it is obvious that the conclusion we are being led to accept is:

> no new drugs should be released for public consumption without a thorough study of their side effects.

The reason given for this is that careful testing of Amotril before it went on sale could have prevented the problems caused by its devastating side effects. In this case, we do not need to tidy up the argument, since it is clear what claim is being made. Moreover, the reason gives good support for the conclusion, provided we assume that one could not find out about a drug's side effects without thorough study, and that it is never worth taking the risk of offering a drug for sale unless we are as certain as we can be that it has no serious side effects.

Here is another example:

> People who diet lose weight. Pavarotti cannot have dieted. He hasn't lost weight.

In this case, we do not have a conclusion indicator such as 'so' or 'therefore', but we do have the word 'cannot'. Is it being used to signal a conclusion? We must consider whether the sentence in which it occurs is the main point which the passage is trying to establish. It seems that the passage is trying to convince us that Pavarotti cannot have dieted, and we seem to have a clear argument if we rearrange it to read:

> People who diet lose weight. Pavarotti hasn't lost weight. Therefore, he cannot have dieted.

This is the most natural way to read the passage.

But suppose we had started out by assuming that the main point which the passage was aiming to get us to accept was that Pavarotti has not lost weight. Then, we would have set out the argument as follows:

> People who diet lose weight. Pavarotti cannot have dieted. Therefore, he hasn't lost weight.

But this is an unnatural reading of the passage, in two respects. First, it would not be natural to use the words 'cannot have dieted' in the second sentence if the meaning it aimed to convey was that Pavarotti has been unable to diet. Second, even if we replaced 'cannot have dieted' with 'has been unable to diet', the first two sentences would be insufficient to establish the conclusion, since Pavarotti may have lost weight by some means other than dieting, for example by taking exercise. Moreover, the kind of evidence which one would have to use in order to establish that Pavarotti had not lost weight would be evidence, not about whether or not he had dieted, but about what he weighed in the past compared with what he weighs now.

Here is another example in which there are no conclusion indicators such as 'so' and 'therefore':

> We need to make rail travel more attractive to travellers. There are so many cars on the roads that the environment and human safety are under threat. Rail travel should be made cheaper. Everyone wants the roads to be less crowded, but they still want the convenience of being able to travel by road themselves. People will not abandon the car in favour of the train without some new incentive.

What is the main point which this piece of reasoning tries to get us to accept? Clearly it is concerned with suggesting a way of getting people to switch from using cars to using trains, on the grounds that it would be a good thing if people did make this switch. We could summarise the passage as follows:

> Because the large numbers of cars on the roads are bad for the environment and human safety, and because people will not abandon the car in favour of the train without some new incentive, we need to make rail travel more attractive. So, rail travel should be made cheaper.

Notice that the word 'should' appears in the conclusion. This may have helped you to see which sentence was the conclusion. Now that we can see more clearly what the argument is, we may question whether it is a good argument. For example, is it the cost of rail travel which deters motorists from switching to using trains, or is it because rail travel is less convenient? Would reducing rail fares really make a difference? Are there any alternative measures which would better achieve the desired effect? Setting out the argument in this way can help us to see what questions we need to ask when we begin to evaluate arguments.

Judging whether a passage contains an argument

Sometimes the subject matter of a passage may make it appear at first sight that an argument is being presented when it is not. Consider these two passages, one of which can be construed as an argument, whereas the other cannot.

> The number of crimes reported to the police is rising. The overall crime rate may not be rising. Traditionally, only a quarter of what most people regard as crime has been notified to the police.

> Most crime is committed by those aged under 21. But most people aged under 21 are not criminals. Some people aged over 21 are persistent offenders.

Let us consider the first passage and ask what main point it is making. Does it try to convince us that the number of crimes reported to the police is rising? It presents no evidence for this, but simply presents it as a fact. Does it try to convince us that traditionally, only a quarter of what most people regard as crime has been notified to the police? Again, no evidence is offered for this. Does it offer evidence for the claim that the overall crime rate may not be rising? Well, it gives us information which shows that this is a possibility. The fact that reported crime is rising may make us suspect that crime is rising overall. But when we are told that there has been a tendency for only a quarter of what is regarded as crime to be reported, we can see that if this tendency has changed in such a way that a greater fraction of what is perceived as crime is now reported, then the overall crime rate may not be rising after all. We can write this argument as follows:

> Traditionally, only a quarter of what most people regard as crime has been notified to the police. So, although the number of crimes reported to the police is rising, the overall crime rate may not be rising.

Notice that the original version of this passage did not contain any of the 'argument indicator' words which we have listed, but it is nevertheless an argument.

Now let us look at the second passage. What does it aim to get us to believe? It presents three comments about statistics on crime, each of which, in a sense, it aims to get us to believe, since it asserts them as being true. However, it does not have a single major point to make, in the sense that none of the statements supports any of the others. You will see this if you try for yourself writing out the three possible ways of treating one of the statements as a conclusion. So this is a passage in which three pieces of information about the same subject-matter are not linked in any process of reasoning; but because of the kind of information presented, that is to say, because it refers to statistics, we may at first be tempted to think of it as an argument, because the use of statistics is a common move in argument. We need to be aware, then, that argument is not just a matter of presenting information – it is, rather, a matter of presenting a conclusion based on information or reasons.

Summary: Is it an argument?

Here is a summary of the steps to take when trying to assess whether a passage is an argument.

1 Look for *conclusion indicator* words, i.e. words such as 'so', 'therefore', 'must', 'cannot', 'should'.

2 If there are no *conclusion indicator* words, look at each sentence in turn and ask, 'Does the rest of the passage give any extra information which tells me why I should believe this?' If the answer is 'No', then this sentence is not a conclusion. If the answer is 'Yes', then the sentence is a conclusion.

3 If none of the sentences in a passage is a conclusion, then the passage is not an argument: *no conclusion, no argument.* If one of the sentences in a passage is a conclusion supported by a reason or reasons in the rest of the passage, then the passage is an argument.

4 When you have found a conclusion in a passage, rewrite the passage with the conclusion at the end, introduced by 'So'. Read through this re-written passage to check that it makes sense. If it does, then you can be certain that this passage is an argument.

Do not worry at this stage about whether the reasons are true, or about whether they give conclusive support to the conclusion.

Exercice 1: Identifying arguments and conclusions

For each of the following passages:

    (a)   decide whether it is an argument;

    (b)   if it is an argument, say what the conclusion is.

1   Pets are good for you. Research has shown that pet owners are less likely than other people to be depressed or to suffer from high blood pressure.

2   A disease found in the faeces of cats can cause miscarriages if it infects pregnant women. Most cat owners are probably immune to this disease. Rabbits can spread listeriosis and salmonella.

3   Children who are good at spelling usually have a good visual memory. Poor spellers have not learnt to look at words carefully. Practice in reading does not necessarily help poor spellers.

4   Millions of pounds of public money are spent defending riverside farmland from flooding. Some of this money should be given to farmers to compensate them for taking such land out of production. This would save money and would benefit the environment, since if rivers were allowed to flood, their natural flood plains would provide wetland meadows and woodland rich in wildlife.

5   This year the incidence of gale force winds in some parts of Britain has been very high. The driest months were January, February and March. July was very wet, and average temperatures were lower than in July last year.

6   The North American Wildlife Federation, which sponsors an annual watch for endangered species, reports that sightings of the bald eagle between 1978 and 1979 increased by 35 per cent. In the watch of 1979, 13,127 sightings of bald eagles were reported, 3,400 over the 1978 count. This indicates considerable growth in the bald eagle population.

(Law School Admission Test, 1981)

7   The presence of security cameras has been shown to reduce crime in areas such as shopping malls. But security cameras are not an unqualified success. Law-abiding citizens do not wish to have all their activities observed, and criminals may commit just as much crime, but do so in areas where there are no cameras.

8   We could reduce road accidents by lowering speed limits, and making greater efforts to ensure that such limits are enforced. But, because this would inconvenience the majority who drive safely, this would be an unacceptable solution to the problem of careless drivers who are unsafe at current speed limits.

9   In the Victorian era, cannabis was used to treat all kinds of conditions, such as muscle spasms, menstrual cramps and rheumatism. Now its use, even for medicinal purposes, is illegal. It has been found to be helpful in relieving the symptoms of multiple sclerosis.

10   Some social historians have claimed that the 1914–18 war enhanced the status of women in Britain, because they were able to leave demeaning jobs in domestic service to work in munitions factories, thus gaining independence and a sense of self-worth. However, the work in these factories was unskilled, repetitive and dangerous – not at all the environment to encourage self-belief. And after the war, women workers were told to give up their jobs to returning soldiers. Many simply returned to domestic service. The reality was thus quite different from what some social historians claim.

Answers to Exercise 1 are given on pp. 141–3.

Identifying reasons

We use reasons in a number of ways, for example to support conclusions of arguments, to support recommendations, to explain why something has happened, or why someone has acted in a particular way. This section focuses on the use of reasons to support conclusions of arguments.

If we have identified a conclusion of an argument which has no argument indicator words, then it is likely that we will already have some idea as to what the reasons of the argument are, since in order to identify the conclusion, we will have had to assess which parts of the passage could be taken to give to support to the chosen conclusion – hence which parts are the reasons. This is what you were doing when you worked through Exercise 1. But if we identify the conclusion by the presence of argument indicator words, then we will have to look again at the passage in order to identify the reasons.

Sometimes we will find characteristic words which indicate the presence of reasons, e.g. 'because', 'for', 'since'. For example, our earlier argument about Pavarotti could have read as follows:

> People who diet lose weight. Since Pavarotti hasn't lost weight, he cannot have dieted.

In this example, the word 'Since' signals that 'Pavarotti hasn't lost weight' is being offered as a reason for the conclusion that Pavarotti cannot have dieted. Sometimes a phrase will be used which tells us explicitly that a reason is being offered, a phrase such as 'the reason for this is'; and sometimes reasons are listed, introduced by the words 'first . . . second . . . (and so on)'.

Arguments often use hypothetical or conditional statements as reasons. These are statements which begin with 'If' and which say that something is true, or will be true, or will happen, provided that (on the condition that) something else is true or something else occurs – for example, 'If I read without wearing my glasses, I will get a headache'. When you see a sentence beginning with the word 'If', think about whether this is being offered as one of the reasons for a conclusion. It is important to remember that it is the whole statement which is being presented as a reason. You should not attempt to break the statement down into two reasons. Sometimes an argument has a hypothetical statement for a conclusion, so you cannot just assume that any hypothetical statement is being offered as a reason.

In common with 'conclusion indicator' words, these 'reason indicator' words can be used in ways other than to introduce a reason, so their presence cannot guarantee that a reason is being offered – but it can be a useful clue. Sometimes, however, we will find no such words or phrases, and will have to rely on our understanding of the meaning of the passage. It may be useful to ask yourself, 'What kind of reason would I have to produce in order to provide support for this conclusion?' You should then look in the passage to see if such reasons are offered.

In addition to the hypothetical statements already mentioned, many different kinds of statements can function as reasons. They may be items of common knowledge, general principles, reports of the results of experiments, statistics, and so on. What they have in common is that they are put forward as being true. Not all the reasons offered in an argument can be given support within that argument. That is to say, that arguments have to start somewhere, so every argument must offer at least one basic reason for which no support is offered. Thus those who present arguments will often take as a starting point something which is obviously true, or the truth of which can easily be checked by others. However, this is not always the case. People may present something which is contentious as a basic reason, and they may fail to give support for such a statement precisely in order to conceal the contentious nature of their argument. So the evaluation of reasoning, which will be discussed in the next chapter, will require us to consider whether the basic reasons presented in any argument are true.

The structure of arguments

The reasons in an argument can fit together in a number of ways. Sometimes there may be only one reason supporting a conclusion, for example:

Pavarotti is thinner. So he has probably been dieting.

In our original Pavarotti argument, there are two reasons:

Reason 1: People who diet lose weight.

Reason 2: Pavarotti hasn't lost weight.

These two reasons, taken together, support the conclusion:

Pavarotti cannot have dieted.

Neither reason on its own would be sufficient to support the conclusion. The number of reasons used in this way in an argument need not be limited to two. An argument could have three, four or a whole string of reasons which need to be taken together in order to support the conclusion.

However, sometimes when there are two (or more) reasons, they are offered not as jointly supporting the conclusion, but as independently supporting it, for example:

It is right to ban cigarette advertising because it encourages young people to start smoking. But even if it had no such influence on young people, it would be right to ban it because it could give existing smokers the mistaken impression that their habit is socially acceptable.

In this case, the conclusion that it is right to ban cigarette advertising could be supported either by the claim that it has the adverse effect of encouraging young people to start smoking, or by the claim that it has the adverse effect of making smokers think that their habit is socially acceptable. Unlike the Pavarotti argument, the author of this argument does not regard it as necessary to offer both reasons, and would claim that the argument had established its conclusion if either reason could be shown to be true. But when an argument offers reasons as jointly supporting the conclusion, then evaluating the argument requires an assessment of the truth of all the reasons.

In the two examples we have just presented, it is clear that in one case joint reasons, and in the other case independent reasons, are being offered. But in some arguments it will be debatable whether the reasons are intended to support the conclusion jointly or independently. Consider the following example:

> Our 40,000 GIs stationed in South Korea support a corrupt regime. The savings in dollars which would result from their coming home could make a sizable dent in the projected federal deficit. Furthermore, the Korean conflict ended 30 years ago. Hence it is time we brought our troops home.
>
> (James B. Freeman, *Thinking Logically*, p. 165)

In this case each one of the first three sentences presents a reason for the conclusion, which appears in the last sentence. Because they are all quite strong reasons for the claim that the troops should be brought home, it may be that the author regards them as independently supporting the conclusion. On the other hand, if they are taken jointly, they present a much stronger case for the conclusion. We could interpret the argument either way here, but it should be remembered in cases like this that, provided all the reasons are true, the argument could be judged to be stronger if it is regarded as presenting joint rather than independent reasons.

Arguments can become much more complicated than the above examples. Reasons may be offered for a conclusion which is then used, either on its own or together with one or more other reasons, in order to draw a further conclusion. It is useful to make a distinction in such cases between an *intermediate conclusion* and a *main conclusion*. Here is an example of an argument with an intermediate conclusion.

> A majority of prospective parents would prefer to have sons rather than daughters. So, if people can choose the sex of their child, it is likely that eventually there will be many more males than females in the population. A preponderance of males in the population is likely to produce serious social problems. Therefore, we should discourage the use of techniques which enable people to choose the sex of their child.

The main conclusion here, signalled by 'Therefore', is that

> we should discourage the use of techniques which enable people to choose the sex of their child.

The immediate reasons given (jointly) for this are:

> if people can choose the sex of their child, it is likely that eventually there will be many more males than females in the population,

and

> a preponderance of males in the population is likely to produce serious social problems.

The first of these two reasons is itself a conclusion, signalled by the word 'So', which follows from the basic reason:

> A majority of prospective parents would prefer to have sons rather than daughters.

Thus an analysis of this passage reveals that the first sentence is a *basic reason*, which supports the *intermediate conclusion* expressed in the second sentence, which in turn, taken jointly with the additional reason offered in the third sentence, supports the *main conclusion* in the last sentence. Unfortunately, not all arguments will set out their reasons and conclusions in this obvious order of progression, so you cannot simply take it for granted that basic reasons will always appear at the beginning, with intermediate conclusions in the middle and main conclusion at the end.

We have mentioned two important approaches to identifying the reasons which are being offered in an argument – first, asking what kind of reason could give support to a particular conclusion, and second, attempting to sort out the way in which the reasons in a passage hang together. It may seem that detailed knowledge of the subject matter will be necessary before one can begin to analyse the argument, and no doubt it is true that the more familiar you are with the subject matter, the more readily will you be able to work out the structure of the argument. However, on many topics, most people will be able to go a long way towards understanding arguments which they encounter in newspapers and textbooks, and they will improve at this task with the kind of practice afforded by the following sets of exercises.

Exercise 2: Offering reasons for conclusions

Working with a partner, take it in turns to think of a simple claim which you think you have good reason to believe. (For example, you may think that there should be speed limits lower than 30 mph on housing estates, because cars travelling at 30 mph on streets where children play can easily cause road deaths.) Tell your partner what your 'conclusion' is (in this example 'Speed limits on housing estates should be lower than 30 mph'). Your partner must then try to offer a reason for this. They may not come up with your reason, but they may come up with another good reason. What you are practising in this exercise is thinking about the *relevance* and the *strength* of potential reasons. You may not come up with the strongest reason, but you should aim to produce something which is clearly relevant, and gives some support to the conclusion, rather than being neutral or counting against it.

Exercise 3: Identifying reasons

This exercise also gives you practice in assessing what could count as a reason for a given 'conclusion'. In each question, pick the answer which could be a reason for the conclusion, and say why this is the right answer, and why the other options are wrong. Note that you are not to worry about whether the reason is true. You must just consider whether, if it were true, it would support the conclusion.

1   *Conclusion*: Blood donors should be paid for giving blood.

   (a)   The Blood Donor service is expensive to administer.

   (b)   People who give blood usually do so because they want to help others.

   (c)   There is a shortage of blood donors, and payment would encourage more people to become donors.

2   *Conclusion*: When choosing someone for a job, employers should base their decision on the applicants' personalities, rather than on their skills.

   (a)   Personalities may change over time, and skills go out of date.

    (b)   Skills can easily be taught, but personalities are difficult to change.

    (c)   Some skills cannot be acquired by everyone, but everyone can develop a good personality.

3   *Conclusion*: Light-skinned people should avoid exposure to the sun.

    (a)   Ultra-violet light from the sun can cause skin cancer on light skins.

    (b)   Dark-skinned people do not suffer as a result of exposure to the sun.

    (c)   Light-skinned people can use sun creams in order to avoid sunburn.

4   *Conclusion*: Installing insulation in your house may be economical in the long run.

    (a)   Less fuel is needed to heat a house which has been insulated.

    (b)   In a house which has been insulated the air feels warmer.

    (c)   Some types of insulation cause houses to be damp.

5   *Conclusion*: In order to reduce crime, we should not use imprisonment as a punishment for young offenders.

    (a)   Young offenders could be taught job skills whilst in prison.

    (b)   It would be expensive to build new prisons to relieve prison overcrowding.

    (c)   Young offenders are more likely to re-offend if their punishment has been a term of imprisonment.

6   *Conclusion*: Sam could not have committed the murder.

    (a)   Sally had both the opportunity and a motive to commit the murder.

    (b)   Sam could not have gained anything by committing the murder.

    (c)   Sam was several miles away from the scene of the murder when the victim was stabbed to death.

7   *Conclusion*: A vegetarian diet may be beneficial to health.

    (a)   A vegetarian diet lacks certain important vitamins.

(b)   A vegetarian diet excludes animal fats which can cause heart disease.

(c)   A vegetarian diet excludes fish oil which is thought to be beneficial to health.

8   *Conclusion*: Parents should be strongly advised to have their children vaccinated against polio.

(a)   Some parents think that there is a risk of harmful side effects from the polio vaccine.

(b)   If a substantial percentage of the population is not vaccinated against polio, there will be outbreaks of the disease every few years.

(c)   The risk of becoming infected with polio is very low.

9   *Conclusion*: Those people who die from drowning are more likely to be swimmers than to be non-swimmers.

(a)   People who cannot swim are much more likely than swimmers to avoid risky water sports.

(b)   Many deaths from drowning occur because people on boating holidays fail to wear life-jackets.

(c)   Even those who can swim may panic if they fall into the sea or a river.

10   *Conclusion*: Some types of chewing-gum are bad for the teeth.

(a)   Some chewing-gums are sweetened with sorbitol, which helps to neutralise tooth-rotting acids.

(b)   The action of chewing gum can get rid of particles of sugar trapped between the teeth.

(c)   Some chewing-gums are sweetened with sugar, which causes tooth decay.

Answers to Exercise 3 are given on pp. 143–6.

Exercise 4: Identifying parts of an argument

For each of the following arguments, identify the main conclusion and the reasons. Say whether there are any intermediate conclusions. Say whether the reasons are intended to support the conclusion jointly or independently.

1   There's no good reason to object to paying for admission to museums and art galleries. After all, you have to pay to go to the theatre or to listen to a concert.

2   A study by psychiatrists at the Royal Free Hospital in London compared treatments for two groups of about seventy patients suffering from depression. In one group, patients were given twelve sessions of psychotherapy; in the other, they were given routine care from their general practitioner. They all improved significantly over the next nine months, and there were no differences between the two groups in the rate and extent of improvement. Psychotherapy is thus no more effective than chatting with your GP.

3   The one-third of people who smoke in public places are subjecting the rest of us to discomfort. What is more, they are putting our health at risk, because 'passive' smoking causes cancer. That is why it is time to ban smoking in public places.

4   Testing drugs on animals cannot give us the information we need in order to assess safety for humans, because animals are too different from humans. The evidence for this is that some drugs which appeared safe in animal tests have been harmful to humans, and that aspirin and penicillin are poisonous to cats.

5   The birth rate in European countries is declining very fast. This means that even though people are living longer, eventually the size of the population will fall, and there will be fewer and fewer people of working age to sustain an ageing population. Either it will be necessary to raise the retirement age, or younger people will have to increase their productivity at work.

6   The introduction of tests on drivers for drugs such as cannabis is being considered, and it has been suggested that a zero limit may

be set. The result would be that someone with even a small amount of cannabis in the bloodstream could be prosecuted. This would be unfair because some people whose driving was not impaired could be prosecuted, since cannabis can remain in the bloodstream for up to four months. So if drug tests are introduced, the limit should not be set at zero.

7   It is clear that global warming is occurring, but we cannot be confident that it is caused by the burning of fossil fuels which produce high levels of carbon dioxide. The earth has experienced warmer climates and higher levels of carbon dioxide in previous ages, long before the current high level of fuel use.

8   Smoking related illnesses don't really cost the state as much as is often claimed. If no one smoked, the revenue from taxes would be massively reduced, and many smokers will die before collecting their full share of health and retirement benefits.

9   Transplanting animal organs into humans should not be allowed. These transplants are expensive to perform, and the risk of animal diseases being transmitted to humans cannot be ruled out. It should be possible to solve the shortfall of organs available for transplant by persuading more people to carry organ donor cards. A human organ must give a human being a better chance of survival.

10   [If killing an animal infringes its rights, then] never may we destroy, for our convenience, some of a litter of puppies, or open a score of oysters when nineteen would have sufficed, or light a candle in a summer evening for mere pleasure, lest some hapless moth should rush to an untimely end. Nay, we must not even take a walk, with the certainty of crushing many an insect in our path, unless for really important business! Surely all this is childish. In the absolute hopelessness of drawing a line anywhere, I conclude that man has an *absolute* right to inflict death on animals, without assigning any reason, provided that it be a painless death, but that any infliction of pain needs its special justification.

(Lewis Carroll, 'Some popular fallacies about vivisection', in *The Complete Works of Lewis Carroll*. Nonesuch, 1939, p. 1072 – emphasis in original)

Answers to Exercise 4 are given on pp. 146–52.

Exercise 5: Thinking about assumptions

Here is a slightly longer passage of reasoning taken from an article in a newspaper, discussing whether Bill Clinton, who was the President of the United States from 1992 until 2000, should be criticised for his alleged sexual involvements with women other than his wife. The article was written some years before Clinton's liaison with Monica Lewinsky – an affair to which he eventually admitted, after having lied on oath about it. The following points may make it easier to understand the passage:

- The author uses the word 'syllogism' in the second sentence, but it is used inaccurately. A syllogism is a particular form of argument. What the author describes as a syllogism is simply a hypothetical statement.
- In the first paragraph the author refers to Richard Nixon, a former President of the United States, and says that 'the American people could not be sure where he was during the day'. This is a reference to the widespread perception of Nixon as being an untrustworthy politician. His nickname was 'Tricky Dickie'.

Now read the passage, say what you think is its main conclusion, and write down a list of assumptions which you think it makes.

Two justifications are generally given for the examination of a politician's sex life. The first is the prissy syllogism that 'if a man would cheat on his wife, he would cheat on his country'. But Gerry Ford and Jimmy Carter were, by most accounts, strong husbands but weak Presidents. I would guess that Pat Nixon knew where Dick was every night. The problem was that the American people could not be sure where he was during the day. Conversely, it is a sad but obvious fact that, to many of those men to whom he gave unusual political nous, God handed out too much testosterone as well.

The second excuse for prurience towards rulers is that leaders, tacitly or explicitly, set examples to the nation and thus their own slips from grace are hypocritical. But Bill Clinton, unlike many senior US politicians, has never publicly claimed that he has led an entirely decent life.

And if the US does wish to impose strict standards of sexual morality on its leaders, then it must properly address the Kennedy paradox. A month ago in Dallas, I watched people weep and cross themselves at the minute of the 30th anniversary of JFK's assassination. If only he had lived, they said then, and millions of middle-aged Americans say it daily. They construct a cult of stolen greatness. But if JFK had lived, he would have been trashed weekly by bimbo anecdotes in the supermarket magazines. If he had run for President in the Eighties, he wouldn't have got beyond New Hampshire before the first high-heel fell on television.

So we must tell the snipers not to fire at Bill Clinton [because of his sex life].

(Mark Lawson, *The Independent*, 30 December 1993, adapted)

Identifying assumptions

We have discussed the two most basic components of arguments – reasons and conclusions – but our understanding of arguments will not be complete unless we can recognise the assumptions upon which an argument relies.

Defining 'assumption'

In order to clarify what is meant by the word 'assumption' in the context of reasoning, let us first consider what we might mean in everyday conversation by talking about 'assuming' something. Suppose you tell me that you are going to the post office before lunch, and I say, 'Take the car, because it will take you too long to walk'. You might reply, 'You're assuming it will take me too long to walk, but you're wrong'. Here you would be referring to something which I have just stated, and telling me that I was mistaken. Hence, everyday usage of the term 'assumption' can imply that an assumption is something which is explicitly asserted, but is not, or may not be, true. One connotation of 'assumption', as people normally use the word, is of a belief that we hold in the absence of strong evidence for its truth – that is to say that the term may mark a distinction between what is known and what is merely believed.

If we interpret the term 'assumption' in this way, we might think that 'assumption' can refer to reasons and conclusions of arguments – that is, to things which have been stated but which may or may not be true. However, those concerned with argument analysis typically make a distinction between reasons, conclusions and *assumptions* in an argument, and we shall be accepting this distinction here. Moreover, our use of the word will *not* imply a distinction between what is known and what is merely believed.

For the purpose of our discussion of assumptions in reasoning, we shall use the word 'assumption' to mean something which is taken for granted, but not stated – something which is implicit rather than explicit. It is the fact that an assumption is unstated which distinguishes it from a reason. There may, or may not, be strong evidence for the truth of an assumption of an argument, and this is a characteristic which it has in common with a reason.

Sometimes in the process of evaluating arguments, the term *presupposition* is used instead of *assumption*. We prefer the term assumption, because of the possibility of confusion between 'presupposing' and 'supposing'. Usually when arguments tell us to '*suppose* that x is true', they are neither stating nor assuming that x *is* true; they are merely exploring what would follow from the truth of x, and often they are doing this precisely in order to show that x must be false. So we must not take the presence of the word 'suppose' in an argument to indicate that an assumption is being made. Indeed, since we are using the term 'assumption' to denote something which is not stated, there are no special words in arguments which are used to indicate the presence of this kind of assumption.

In the sense of 'assumption' set out above, arguments have many assumptions. For each argument we encounter, there will be a whole host of shared background information – for example, the meanings of the words in which the argument is expressed, and general knowledge which gives support to the reasons which are presented. Sometimes these assumptions will be so uncontentious that we will not be interested in making them explicit. Sometimes, however, we will suspect that an argument rests upon a dubious assumption, and it will be important for us to express exactly what that assumption is in order to assess the argument.

We shall say more later about assumptions concerning the meanings of words, assumptions about analogous or comparable situations, and assumptions concerning the appropriateness of a given explanation. But for this chapter, we shall focus on the following two important ways in which assumptions function in an argument; first, in giving support to the basic reasons presented in the argument; second, as a missing step within the argument – perhaps as an additional reason which must be added to the stated reasons in order for the conclusion to be established, or perhaps as an intermediate conclusion which is supported by the reasons, and in turn supports the main conclusion. Let us explore these two uses of assumptions by looking at some examples.

Assumptions underlying basic reasons

The following argument (used in a slightly different form on p. 7 as an example of an argument without a conclusion indicator word) provides an example of the use of an assumption in the first sense, that is to say as something which is intended to support one of the basic reasons of the argument.

> One-third of the population still smokes. Everyone must know that smoking causes lung cancer and heart disease. So, knowing the dangers of smoking is not sufficient to stop people from smoking.

This piece of reasoning presents two (basic) reasons for its conclusion:

> *Reason 1*: One-third of the population still smokes.
>
> *Reason 2*: Everyone must know that smoking causes lung cancer and heart disease.

In such arguments, the basic reasons may be well-established facts, or they may make the kind of factual claim which we could easily check. Reason 1 seems to be of this nature – that is to say that either it is a generally accepted fact, backed up by reliable statistics, or the author of the argument has made an error about the statistics, and the fraction of the population who smoke is something other than one-third. But we do not need to worry about the reasonableness or unreasonableness of assumptions in relation to Reason 1, because we would be able to seek confirmation as to the correct figure, and in any case, the exact figure is not crucial to establishing the conclusion. Provided that *some* of the population still smoke – and our own experience confirms the truth of this – and provided Reason 2 is true, then Reason 1, taken together with Reason 2, gives support to the conclusion.

Reason 2, however, seems a less straightforward factual claim than Reason 1. What lends support to this statement? The claim that 'everyone *must* know . . .' suggests that there is an underlying reason for expecting people to be well-informed on this topic, and the obvious candidate is that there has been widespread publicity on the dangers to health of smoking – on television, in newspapers and by means of posters in the waiting rooms of doctors and hospitals. Yet, the move from the doubtless true claim that there has been publicity about the dangers – to the further claim – that everyone must know about the dangers – depends upon an assumption that everyone has absorbed this information, is capable of understanding the messages which are being put across, and accepts the truth of those messages.

This may seem a reasonable assumption to make, but there may well be those who would wish to challenge it by pointing out that, despite publicity campaigns, some people may not believe that there is a causal link between smoking and ill-health, because they think that the statistics are inconclusive. Even if you do not regard this assumption as controversial, the example illustrates the way in which we can attempt to identify potentially controversial assumptions underlying the basic reasons presented in an argument. Clearly the identification of such assumptions is closely associated with evaluating the truth of reasons, which will be discussed further in the next chapter.

Another example of assumptions which underlie basic reasons is provided by the passage below:

> Occupational accidents will never be eliminated because all human activity entails risk. But the total number of accidents could be greatly reduced, and the surest way of achieving such a reduction is to penalise, with fines or even imprisonment, those employers on whose premises they occur. Such a policy might result in cases of individual injustice, but it would be effective in securing safer workplaces.

Before reading on, ask yourself what this passage is recommending, and why.

The passage is recommending the imposition of penalties on employers on whose premises occupational accidents occur, on the grounds that this would be the best way to reduce the number of such accidents. There is an obvious unstated assumption here that the threat of penalties would influence the behaviour of employers. But there is a further assumption, since the existence of penalties would not reduce the number of accidents if it were beyond the power of employers to prevent some of the accidents which now occur. So the argument assumes that it is possible for employers to take measures which will prevent the occurrence of some accidents.

Both these assumptions function as reasons which need to be taken together in order to support the claim that the threat of penalties would reduce accidents; and both are reasonable assumptions to make. However, even with these assumptions, the conclusion is too strong, since nothing has yet been said to support the idea that introducing penalties is the *surest* way of achieving a reduction in accidents. So there is yet another assumption – that no other method would be as effective in reducing the number of accidents – and this assumption is more controversial than the others, since it may be possible to get employers to take appropriate action by offering them incentives.

Assumptions as unstated reasons or conclusions

The second type of assumption is one which is needed to fill a gap within the argument, either as an additional reason, without which the reasons which *are* offered do not fully support the conclusion, or as a missing link between the reasons and the conclusion. Here is an example of an argument which illustrates the former:

> In tests designed to investigate the effect of a time delay on recalling a list of words, subjects remembered fewer words after a 30-second delay than after a 10-second delay. Therefore, after a 60-second delay, we would expect subjects to remember even fewer words than after a 30-second delay.

Before going on, ask yourself what is being assumed. Write down any assumption you can identify.

The argument gives just one reason for its conclusion that subjects can be expected to remember fewer words after a 60-second delay than after a 30-second delay. The reason is the piece of evidence that fewer words are remembered after 30 seconds than after 10 seconds. But this piece of evidence supports the conclusion only if it is true that the ability to recall goes on declining after a 30-second delay. So the argument is relying on this assumption in order to draw its conclusion. If we did not make this assumption explicit, we might happily accept the conclusion as obviously following from the evidence. Even when the assumption has been identified, we may consider it a reasonable assumption to make. Nevertheless, it is possible that subjects would be able to remember just as many words after 60 seconds as after 30 seconds, perhaps because the number of words still retained in the memory was a manageable number for the memory to hold. Self-respecting psychologists would not be prepared to draw a firm conclusion without carrying out an appropriate further test.

Here is another example in which one of the reasons has been left unstated:

> If cigarette advertising is banned, cigarette manufacturers will save the money they would otherwise have spent on advertising. Thus, in order to compete with each other, they will reduce the price of cigarettes. So, banning cigarette advertising will be likely to lead to an increase in smoking.

Before reading further, think about the reasoning in this passage. What conclusion is it trying to get us to accept? What basic reason does it offer?

Is there an intermediate conclusion? Can you identify a stage in the argument which has not been stated?

The argument starts with a basic reason:

> If cigarette advertising is banned, cigarette manufacturers will save the money they would otherwise have spent on advertising.

From this it draws the conclusion (an intermediate conclusion):

> Thus, in order to compete with each other, they will reduce the price of cigarettes.

It then draws the main conclusion:

> So, banning cigarette advertising will be likely to lead to an increase in smoking.

The main conclusion would not follow from the intermediate conclusion if a reduction in the price of cigarettes made no difference to the numbers of cigarettes bought and smoked. So an assumption underlies this move – that if cigarettes were cheaper, smokers would smoke more, or non-smokers would become smokers. The conclusion does not say exactly what it means by 'an increase in smoking', so we cannot be sure whether the assumption is:

> If cigarettes were cheaper, smokers would smoke more,

or

> If cigarettes were cheaper, more people would smoke,

or perhaps both of these. However, it clearly requires at least one of these assumptions in order to support the conclusion, and perhaps both assumptions are questionable. This is a case of an assumption which, taken together with an intermediate conclusion, gives support to the main conclusion of the argument.

In some pieces of reasoning, an intermediate conclusion may be left unstated. Imagine the following report being made by a policeman to his superior officer about a theft from an art gallery.

> The burglar must have left by the fire escape. This person is not in the building now, but has not been seen leaving the building, and there are guards posted at each entrance.

What intermediate conclusion is the policeman drawing which he has not actually stated? Is this a reasonable conclusion to draw?

The policeman gives three reasons which, taken together, are intended to support the conclusion that the burglar must have left by the fire escape:

Reason 1: This person is not in the building now.

supports the claim that the burglar must have left the building. But

Reason 2: (the person) has not been seen leaving, and

Reason 3: there are guards posted at each entrance.

do not entitle us to conclude that the burglar must have left by the fire escape unless we assume that Reason 3 supports an intermediate conclusion to the effect that no one could leave undetected except by the fire escape. This assumption, taken together with Reasons 1 and 2, give strong support to the conclusion. However, the assumption itself is open to dispute. Perhaps the guards were insufficiently watchful, or failed to recognise the burglar as a burglar, or perhaps it is possible for someone to leave the building undetected through a window on the ground floor.

In the above examples, we have often found that identifying an assumption has led us to question the truth of that assumption, and perhaps to reserve judgement on an argument until we have obtained further evidence or information. But sometimes when we have identified an assumption, we will see that there is no good reason to think it is true, and we will therefore judge the argument to be unsound. Consider the following example:

Some people say that the depiction of violence on television has no effect on viewers' behaviour. However, if what was shown on television did not affect behaviour, television advertising would never influence viewers to buy certain products. But we know that it does. So it cannot be true that television violence does not affect behaviour.

See if you can pick out the missing assumption here, and say what is wrong with it.

At first sight, this looks like a plausible argument, and many people will be tempted to accept that it is successful in establishing its conclusion. Yet, whichever way we interpret it, it rests on a dubious assumption. One way of interpreting it is to see it as relying on the assumption that, on the one hand, the depiction of violence on television and, on the other hand, advertising on television are alike in important ways – indeed, in ways which allow us to conclude that if one affects the behaviour of viewers, the other one must also affect the behaviour of viewers. But the only thing which they have in common which is *mentioned* in the argument is that both are shown on television.

Perhaps they are alike in some respects, for example, in that they are dramatic, and likely to make an impact on viewers in such a way that viewers remember them. But perhaps the differences between them make a difference to their effects on viewers' behaviour. They are different in that programmes depicting violence are not trying to *sell* violence, not trying to make it attractive to the viewer. There may also be a difference in that most people's natural response to violence is not one of approval, whereas they may well approve of and aspire to some of the lifestyles depicted in advertisements. So the assumption that the two are alike in ways which are relevant to their possible effects on viewers' behaviour is questionable.

There are two other possible interpretations of the passage, each of which rests on a dubious assumption. It *may* be suggesting that because television advertising affects viewers' behaviour, *everything* shown on television, including depictions of violence, must affect behaviour. In that case, the dubious assumption is that if one aspect of television output affects behaviour, all aspects must. Alternatively, it *may* be suggesting that the example of advertising demonstrates that *some* things shown on television affect behaviour. In that case, in drawing its conclusion, it relies on the wholly implausible assumption if some things which are shown on television affect behaviour, then violence shown on television must be one of those things.

The discovery that this argument does not give strong support to its conclusion does not establish that its conclusion is false. Perhaps violence shown on television does affect viewers' behaviour, but, if this is so, it is a truth which cannot be established by means of this particular argument. The ability to identify the mistakes in other people's reasoning is a valuable skill which will be discussed in more detail in the next chapter.

The examples discussed above have been of specific assumptions relating to the subject matter of particular arguments. There are some assumptions which form the whole context in which an argument is presented, but which may not be made explicit, so that someone unfamiliar with the context will find it more difficult to understand the argument. Consider the following passage:

> It has been claimed that powdered rhinoceros horn has aphrodisiac properties, but scientists investigating its effects have been unable to find any chemical effect on the human nervous system. Also, an experiment was carried out in which 100 people ate powdered rhinoceros horn, and another 100 people ate powdered rice, without knowing what they were eating. Very many more of those who ate the rice reported feeling an increase

in sexual arousal than did those who ate the rhinoceros horn. This demonstrates that rhinoceros horn probably does not have aphrodisiac properties.

In describing the experiment, and making the claim about what it demonstrates, this argument does not bother to state that powdered rice is not an aphrodisiac. But we can understand that this is being taken for granted, if we reason as follows:

> If rhinoceros horn has aphrodisiac properties, then more people should report an increase in sexual arousal after eating rhinoceros horn than after eating powdered rice, which we know does not have aphrodisiac properties. But this did not happen in the experiment. So rhinoceros horn does not have aphrodisiac properties.

Someone familiar with the way in which such experiments are carried out – the use of a control group of people with which to compare those on whom the rhinoceros horn is tested, the attempt to eliminate irrelevant psychological effects by keeping subjects ignorant of which substance they are eating – will readily understand why the conclusion is being drawn, and will see that there is an unstated assumption that powdered rice is not an aphrodisiac.

Someone unfamiliar with the context of experiments may find it more difficult to understand what is going on. They may, of course, notice that nothing is said about the aphrodisiac properties of powdered rice, and they may reason as follows:

> Powdered rice either does or does not have aphrodisiac properties. If it does, then the experiment cannot tell us whether rhinoceros horn has no aphrodisiac properties or merely weaker aphrodisiac properties than does powdered rice. If it does not, then the experiment *does* indicate that rhinoceros horn does not have aphrodisiac properties, because if it did have such properties, the number of those reporting an increase in sexual arousal should have been higher amongst those who ate rhinoceros horn than amongst those who ate powdered rice.

However, this a complex piece of reasoning, and, rather than hitting upon this, readers of the argument might instead imagine a context in which it is not known by the experimenters whether *either* substance has aphrodisiac properties. They might then conclude that the experiment appeared to indicate that both substances have aphrodisiac properties, although the powdered rice had much stronger aphrodisiac properties than the rhinoceros horn. So they might regard the conclusion of the argument as mistaken, even though, provided one assumes that powdered rice is not an aphrodisiac, it is a reasonable conclusion to draw from the evidence.

This is an example, then, of an argument with a specific unstated assumption, which it will be more difficult to identify if one is unfamiliar with the context – the whole set of background assumptions – in which the argument is set. This indicates the value of understanding certain contexts of arguments, and that it is valuable to ask certain questions about any argument which cites experimental evidence – for example, what is the purpose of any comparison which is being made between different groups of people, what differing conclusions could be drawn on the basis of one set of assumptions as opposed to a conflicting set of assumptions?

We have said little here about assumptions as to the meanings of words and phrases used in reasoning, but we shall discuss this in greater detail in Chapter 5. The following exercises will enable you to practise the skill of identifying assumptions.

Exercise 6: Identifying someone else's assumptions

Sometimes we may find it more difficult to identify the assumptions underlying our own reasoning than to identify the assumptions upon which others are relying. This exercise aims to make you more aware that there may be unstated beliefs in your own reasoning which others would wish to challenge. Suppose, for example, you were to say that the police force should devote more of their time to patrolling on foot in rural areas and suburbs, and, as your reason for believing this, you said that crime has increased in these areas. Someone may point out to you that you are assuming that the presence of policemen on the streets and country lanes can deter potential criminals from committing crimes.

Work with a partner for this exercise. From the following list, choose a statement with which you agree, and give your partner just one reason why you believe this. Your partner must then try to identify any unstated assumptions upon which your view depends.

1 Smoking in public places should be banned.

2 Boxing is a barbaric activity.

3 People should be allowed to hunt foxes.

4 Coarse fishing is a pointless pastime.

5 The older one gets, the wiser one becomes.

---

6   Newly qualified drivers should not be allowed to drive on motor-ways.

7   The pattern of family life has changed in recent years.

8   Schools should be required to provide sex education.

9   Too many new motorways are being built.

10   It was a good idea to set up the National Lottery.

You can continue this exercise choosing your own topics. Choose something which is of general interest, but about which you know people tend to disagree.

Exercise 7: Identifying assumptions in arguments

For each of the following passages, identify any unstated assumptions, and say whether they are assumptions which underlie a basic reason, or assumptions which function as an additional reason, or assumptions which function as an intermediate conclusion.

1   Men are generally better than women at what psychologists call 'target-directed motor skills', but what the rest of us call 'playing darts'. Many people would say that this is not due to innate biological differences in the brain, but is due to the fact that upbringing gives boys more opportunities to practise these skills. But there must be some innate difference, because even three-year-old boys are better than girls of the same age at target skills.

2   Allowing parents to choose the sex of their children could have serious social costs. There would be a higher percentage of males who were unable to find a female partner. Also, since it is true that 90 per cent of violent crimes are committed by men, the number of violent crimes would rise.

3   When people live in a house for a long period of time, they develop a strong commitment to the local neighbourhood. So the continued fall in house prices may have a beneficial effect. The middle classes will become enthusiastic campaigners for better schools, and against vandalism, traffic congestion and noisy neighbours.

4   If the money has been stolen, someone must have disabled the alarm system, because the alarm easily wakes me if it goes off. So the culprit must be a member of the security firm which installed the alarm.

5   The campaign to eradicate measles has been so successful that many doctors have never seen an actual case. Ironically, this puts those few people who do contract the disease in greater danger than they would have been before. The disease can cause serious complications, and it is difficult to diagnose without previous experience because the symptoms are similar to those of several other diseases.
(Law School Admission Test, December 1984)

6   There is a much higher incidence of heart attack and death from heart disease among heavy cigarette smokers than among people who do not smoke. It has been thought that nicotine was responsible for the development of atherosclerotic disease in smokers. It now seems that the real culprit is carbon monoxide. In experiments, animals exposed to carbon monoxide for several months show changes in the arterial walls that are indistinguishable from atherosclerosis.
(Law School Admission Test, March 1985)

7   Patients on the point of death, who either died shortly afterwards or were revived, have often reported visions of places of exquisite beauty, intense feelings of peace and joy, and encounters with loved ones who had predeceased them. These experiences clearly suggest that there is life after death. Skeptics often claim that such phenomena are caused by changes in the brain that precede death, because these phenomena resemble certain altered states of consciousness that can be induced by drugs or organic brain disease. This objection fails, however, because most of the patients whose experiences of this nature have been reported were neither drugged nor suffering from brain disease.
(Law School Admission Test, October 1985)

8   The growth in the urban population of the US has put increasing pressure on farmers to produce more food. Farmers have responded by adopting labour saving technology that has resulted in a further displacement of population to cities. As a result, the farm population,

formerly a dominant pressure group in national politics, has lost political power.

(Law School Admission Test, February 1983)

9 Human beings have the power either to preserve or to destroy wild plant species. Most of the wonder drugs of the past fifty years have come from wild plants. If those plants had not existed, medicine could not have progressed as it has, and many human lives would have been lost. It is therefore important for the future of medicine that we should preserve wild plant species.

10 Thirty years ago the numbers of British people taking holidays in foreign countries were very small compared with the large numbers of them travelling abroad for holidays now. Foreign travel is, and always has been, expensive. So British people must on average have more money to spend now than they did thirty years ago.

Answers to Exercise 7 are given on pp. 152–6.

Exercise 8: Re-working Exercise 5

Re-read the passage for Exercise 5 (p. 24). Identify its conclusion, reasons and unstated assumptions. Compare the list which you originally wrote for Exercise 5 with the unstated assumptions which you have now identified.

Answers to Exercise 8 are given on pp. 156–9.

Chapter 2

Evaluating reasoning

Parts of an argument

Let us remind ourselves of the most important points covered in the last chapter:

1 An *argument* offers a *reason* or reasons in support of a *conclusion.*
2 Conclusions may
   • state a supposed fact (for example, 'It is dangerous to drive a car after drinking alcohol'); or
   • make a recommendation (for example, 'You ought not to drive your car').
3 Some arguments introduce their conclusion with the word 'so' or the word 'therefore'; some arguments do not contain the words 'so' or 'therefore'.
4 A conclusion does not have to be the last statement in the argument. Conclusions can appear anywhere in the argument.
5 An argument can have *unstated assumptions*, that is, items of information, or ideas, which are not explicitly stated in the argument, but upon which the argument relies in order to draw its conclusion
6 Arguments can have many different structures, for example:
   • one reason supporting a conclusion;
   • two or more reasons which, taken together, support the conclusion;
   • two or more reasons, each of which independently supports the conclusion; or

- a reason, or reasons, which support an intermediate conclusion, which is then used, either on its own, or with other reasons to support a main conclusion.

Once we understand both the explicit and the implicit reasoning in a passage, we are in a position to assess whether the reasoning is good. There are two questions involved in this assessment:

- Are the reasons (and any unstated assumptions) true?
- Does the main conclusion (and any intermediate conclusion) follow from the reasons given for it?

The answer to both of these questions must be 'yes' in order for an argument to be a good argument. Let us illustrate this with some simple examples. Here is the first one:

> Everyone who exercises regularly in the gym has well-developed muscles. So if Mel doesn't have well-developed muscles, it can't be true that she's exercising regularly in the gym.

In this argument, if the reason is false – that is, if it isn't true that everyone who exercises regularly in the gym has well-developed muscles – then the argument cannot establish that someone without well-developed muscles does not exercise regularly in the gym. So it is clear that we need to know whether the reason is true in order to know whether we should accept the conclusion. If the reason were true, then, in this example, we would have a good argument, since the reason supports the conclusion.

By contrast, in our second example the reason does not support the conclusion:

> Everyone who exercises regularly in the gym has well-developed muscles. So if Mel has well-developed muscles, she must be exercising regularly in the gym.

Here, even if the reason is true, the conclusion is not established, since the reason establishes only that all those who exercise regularly in the gym have well-developed muscles, and *not* that no one else has well-developed muscles. This example illustrates that our second question – as to whether the conclusion follows from the reasons given for it – is also crucial to any assessment of an argument.

Evaluating the truth of reasons and assumptions

Common knowledge

It is obvious that no one will be in a position to know whether all the reasons presented in all the arguments that they may encounter are true. However, we all have a share in a body of common knowledge, many of us have detailed knowledge about our particular field of work or study, and we have some ideas about whom to trust to give us correct information on subjects which are less familiar to us.

Common knowledge can take us a long way in assessing many of the short arguments we looked at earlier. For example, we noted (p. 27) that in the following argument, it was easy for us to assess the first of the reasons:

> One-third of the population still smokes. Everyone must know that smoking causes lung cancer and heart disease. So, knowing the dangers of smoking is not sufficient to stop people from smoking.

We may not know the accuracy of the claim that one-third of the population still smokes. But we know that quite a number of people still smoke, because we see them doing so; and the argument only needs to establish that *some* people still smoke, despite knowing the dangers. The second reason – that everyone must know the effects of smoking – is more difficult to assess. We observed that it depends upon an assumption that the publicity about the dangers of smoking has been absorbed by everyone,

Perhaps one way to find out if this is so would be to interview smokers in order to discover whether they believe that smoking is dangerous to health. If we found that many smokers do not believe this, we would have produced a piece of additional evidence which would cast doubt on the conclusion. (We shall say more about evaluating additional evidence in a later section.)

We may sometimes need to assess the truth of statements by relying on other people as authorities, perhaps because being certain about the truth of a particular statement depends upon direct experience, which we lack. For example, we may find ourselves as members of a jury having to assess the evidence of eye witnesses to a crime. We do not have the direct experience of what happened, and we may hear two witnesses describing the events in two conflicting ways. Another case in which we may have to rely on authorities is where knowledge depends upon expertise, which we ourselves lack. We may, for example, have to rely on the authority of scientists, because we lack the expertise to carry out for ourselves the experiments which they claim establish the truth of something. Although we cannot guarantee that by relying on the authority of others, we will never be mistaken about anything, there are certain criteria we can use in order to minimise the chances of being misled by other people.

Reliability of authorities

If one of your acquaintances has a record of being untruthful, then you are much more cautious about accepting their statements as true than you would be about believing someone who you thought had never lied to you. For example, if someone who always exaggerates about his success with women tells you that at last night's disco several women chatted him up, you will be inclined to be sceptical. The habitual liar is an obvious case of someone whose statements are unreliable. In assessing the reliability of authorities, we have to think about the circumstances which could make it likely that what someone said was untrue.

Of course, people who are not habitual liars may deceive others on occasions. They may do so because they stand to lose a great deal – money, respect or reputation – by telling the truth. So when we have to make judgements about the reliability of people we know to be generally truthful, and about people with whom we are not acquainted, we should bear this consideration in mind. That is not to say that we should assume people are being untruthful, simply because it would be damaging to them if others believed the opposite of what they say. But when we have to judge between two conflicting pieces of information from two different people, we should consider whether one of those people has a vested interest in making us believe what they say. For example, if an adult discovers two children fighting, then each child has a vested interest in claiming that the other started the fight. But the evidence of a third child who observed the fight, but knows neither of the protagonists, could be taken to be more reliable in these circumstances.

If someone was not in a position to have the relevant knowledge about the subject under discussion, then it would be merely accidental if their statements about the subject were true. There are a number of circumstances which prevent people from having the relevant knowledge. The subject under discussion may be a highly specialised subject which is understood only by those who have had appropriate education or training. We would not expect reliable information on brain surgery to be given by people who have had absolutely no medical training. This is why in many areas of knowledge, we have to rely on what experts say. It is important to note, however, that being an expert, no matter how eminent, in one field, does not confer reliability on topics beyond one's area of expertise.

People who are not experts can read about specialised subjects, and pass on information to us about such subjects, so we do not have to disbelieve people simply because they are not experts. But we would be wise to ask the source of their information. For example, if someone told us that they had read that a new car had better safety features than any other model, we should regard the information as more reliable if it came from a consumer magazine or a motoring association than if it was a report of a comment made by a famous person who owned such a car.

Another circumstance in which someone would not be in a position to have the relevant knowledge would be where eye-witness testimony was crucial, and the person could not have seen clearly what happened – perhaps because of poor eyesight, or perhaps because he or she did not have a clear line of vision on the incident. In the case of a road accident, for example, we would expect to get a more accurate account of what happened from someone with good vision who was close to the accident and whose view was not obscured in any way, than from someone with poor eyesight, or who was at some distance from the accident, or who was viewing it from an angle, or through trees. Similar considerations would apply in the case of information dependent upon hearing rather than vision.

Someone who aims to tell the truth, and who is in a position to have the relevant knowledge may nevertheless be unreliable because of circumstances which interfere with the accuracy of his or her judgement. For example, emotional stress, drugs and alcohol can affect our perceptions. We can be distracted by other events which are happening concurrently. A parent with fractious children in the car may notice less about a road accident than someone who is travelling alone. We can forget important aspects of what has happened, particularly if some time elapses before we report an incident. In the case of people gathering and assessing evidence, as for example scientists and psychologists do, the accuracy of their observations and interpretations can be affected by their strong expectation of a particular result, or their strong desire to have a particular theory confirmed.

Sometimes when we have evidence from more than one source, we find that two (or more) people agree in their descriptions of events – that is to say, their evidence *corroborates* the statements of others. In these circumstances, unless there is any reason to think that the witnesses are attempting to mislead us, or any reason to think that one witness has attempted to influence others, we should regard corroboration as confirming the reliability of evidence.

Summary: Reliability of evidence/authorities

Here is a summary of the important questions to ask yourself about the reliability of evidence and of authorities.

1 *Is this person likely to be telling a lie, to be failing to give full relevant information, or to be attempting to mislead?*
  - do they have a record of being untruthful?
  - do they have a reason for being untruthful?
  (Would they gain something very important by deceiving me?)
  (Would they lose something very important by telling the truth?)
2 *Is this person in a position to have the relevant knowledge?*
  - If expert knowledge is involved, are they an expert, or have they been informed by an expert?
  - If first-hand experience is important, were they in a position to have that experience?
  (If observation is involved, could they see and hear clearly?)
3 *Are there any factors which would interfere with the accuracy of this person's judgement?*
  - Was, or is, the person under emotional stress?
  - Was, or is, the person under the influence of alcohol or drugs?
  - Was the person likely to have been distracted by other events?
  - Does the person have a strong desire or incentive to believe one version of events, or one explanation, rather than another?
  - In the case of first-hand experience of an event, was information obtained from the person immediately following the event?
4 Is there evidence from another source which corroborates this person's statement?

Evaluating support for conclusions

You have already had some practice in judging whether a conclusion follows from, or is supported by, a given reason. This was what Exercise 3 involved, since you were asked to pick out from three statements the one which could be a reason for the conclusion. When trying to decide whether conclusions of arguments are established by the reasons presented, you are essentially doing the same thing as you did for Exercise 3, but you may have to take into account more than one reason. You may also have to assess a chain of reasoning, which could involve judging whether an intermediate conclusion follows from some basic reasons, and also whether it in turn supports a main conclusion.

A reason will not support a conclusion if it is not *relevant* to the conclusion. This may seem very obvious, since if a reason is concerned with some topic completely unrelated to the subject matter of the conclusion, it would be clearly mistaken to think that the reason could support the conclusion. However, when we talk about a reason being *relevant* to the conclusion, we do not simply mean that it is about the same topic. What we mean is that the reason, if true, *makes a difference* to the acceptability of the conclusion. Relevance in this sense does not necessarily mean that a *relevant* statement *supports* a conclusion. A statement could be relevant and yet count against the conclusion. If we look again at one of the questions from Exercise 3 on p. 19, we can see an example of this:

Conclusion: Blood donors should be paid for giving blood.

Which of the following, if true, could be a reason for the above conclusion?

(a) The Blood Donor service is expensive to administer.
(b) People who give blood usually do so because they want to help others.
(c) There is a shortage of blood donors, and payment would encourage more people to become donors.

The correct answer to this question is (c), which supports the conclusion by showing that if payment were offered to blood donors, this could remedy the shortage of donors. But (a) is also relevant to the conclusion, in the sense that it has some bearing on the recommendation to pay blood donors. If the blood donor service is already expensive to administer, then this may be a reason for rejecting the recommendation. Hence (a) does not support the conclusion, it counts against it.

You may find it useful to think about whether reasons are relevant, because if you can quickly spot that a reason is irrelevant, then you will know that it does not support the conclusion. However, the above example shows that the judgement that a reason is relevant is not sufficient to tell you that the reason supports the conclusion. You will still have to think about the way in which it has a bearing on the conclusion.

The strength of support which reasons provide for a conclusion can vary. In the argument on p. 40, for example, the reason gives the strongest possible support to the conclusion. The argument says:

Everyone who exercises regularly in the gym has well-developed muscles. So if Mel doesn't have well-developed muscles, it can't be true that she's exercising regularly in the gym.

In this case, if the reason is true, the conclusion *must* be true. Other arguments may provide less strong support, and nevertheless be good arguments. We can have good reason for believing that something will happen in the future based on evidence from the past, or for believing that what is known to be true of a number of cases will be true of another similar case. For example, we could have good reason to believe that a new car will be reliable, based on the knowledge that most other cars of that model have been reliable. It is not possible to be precise about degrees of strength of support, and in many cases we may need to find out more about the context of an argument in order to assess whether the reasons give strong, fairly strong or only weak support for the conclusion.

In addition to differences in the strength of arguments, there are also different ways in which reasons can support their conclusions; arguments may present past experience as evidence for their conclusion, they may use analogies (i.e. draw their conclusions on the basis of what is true of similar cases), they may refer to statistics, or to results of experiments in science or studies in psychology or sociology, they may base their conclusions on general principles. In relation to all these kinds of reasons, it is useful to ask yourself the following questions about the argument.

1　Are the reasons/evidence relevant to the conclusion?
2　If so, do the reasons/evidence provide a good basis for accepting the conclusion?
3　If the conclusion recommends some action or policy, would it be reasonable to act on the basis of the reasons/evidence? In order to answer this question, you will need to consider the following points:
   • would the recommended policy or action be likely to achieve the desired aim?
   • would it have some undesirable effects?
   • are there other, possibly better, ways of achieving the aim?
4　Can I think of any other evidence, not mentioned in the argument, which would weaken or strengthen the conclusion?

Let's put this into practice with a few examples. Consider the following argument:

> You ought to take a Happitum travel sickness pill when you go on the ferry. They are very effective against sea-sickness, and you have always been sick in the past when you've travelled by sea.

In this example, it is easy to see that the reasons, if true, give fairly strong support to the conclusion. If you have always been sick on sea crossings, then past experience suggests that you are likely to be sick this time, unless you can prevent this, perhaps by taking some effective drug. So it would be reasonable to act on the evidence that Happitum is effective in preventing sea-sickness. Of course, there may be other considerations, not mentioned in the argument, which would count against the conclusion. If, for example, Happitum had serious side-effects, then it may be more sensible to endure sea-sickness rather than risk ill-health from the drug. Or maybe there are techniques for combating sea-sickness (for example, staying on deck and breathing deeply), which are likely to be effective, and which are less unpleasant than taking a drug.

Here is another example:

> New drugs have been developed which can combat the body's tendency to reject transplanted organs. In the past, most of the deaths which have occurred shortly after heart transplant operations have been due to rejection. So it is likely that these new drugs will improve the survival rate of heart transplant patients.

Are the reasons relevant to the conclusion? Yes, since if most deaths of heart transplant patients have been caused by organ rejection, then the use of drugs which counteract rejection is likely to enable some patients to survive who would have died without the drugs. The reasons are not only relevant to the conclusion, they give it strong support, since if some patients survive who would otherwise have died, this means that the survival rate is higher. There may, of course, be evidence not presented here which would count against the conclusion, for example, if the drugs were highly toxic. But on the assumption that the drugs have been tested for toxicity, and found to be relatively safe, we can regard the conclusion as well supported by the reasons.

Let's look at one more example:

> We could introduce a much more difficult written test for learner drivers in the UK but, since this would not improve their driving skills, it would not result in a lower accident rate amongst young drivers. In Portugal, learner drivers must have five weeks' theoretical instruction and a stiff examination before they are legally entitled to touch the wheel, but this does not result in a low accident rate amongst young newly qualified drivers. They soon forget about the test once they start to drive. All it indicates is that candidates can read and write. It has no bearing on their ability to drive.

This argument uses evidence from Portugal in order to draw a conclusion about what would be likely to happen in the UK. Its major reasons:

> In Portugal, learner drivers must have five weeks' theoretical instruction and a stiff examination before they are legally entitled to touch the wheel, but this does not result in a low accident rate amongst new drivers.

and

> [the test] has no bearing on their ability to drive.

are offered in support of an intermediate conclusion that:

> [Introducing] a much more difficult written test for learner drivers in the UK . . . would not improve their driving skills.

which in turn is offered to support the main conclusion that:

> [Introducing] a much more difficult written test for learner drivers in the UK . . . would not result in a lower accident rate amongst young drivers.

We need to ask first whether the reasons are relevant to the conclusion. Remember that we are not questioning the truth of the reasons at this stage. We are considering whether, assuming the reasons to be true, they support the conclusion.

So, if it's true that the stiff written examination in Portugal does not produce a low accident rate amongst new drivers, and that it has no bearing on driving ability, is this relevant to the claim that such an examination in the UK would have no impact on the accident rate amongst drivers aged 17 to 21? Well it certainly is a piece of evidence which is worth taking into account, since it is one example of a test which has not had the result which is perhaps hoped for in the UK. But when we consider whether the evidence gives us sufficient basis for accepting and acting upon the conclusion, a number of further questions come to mind. Is there any evidence from other countries besides Portugal? Are the accidents in this age group (both in the UK and in Portugal) attributable mainly to the driver's lack of skill, or perhaps to the driver's reckless attitude? Are there any cultural differences which might give a test greater impact on attitudes amongst young drivers in the UK than it has amongst their counterparts in Portugal? There is insufficient evidence in this argument to give very strong support to the conclusion.

Identifying flaws in reasoning

Some arguments give either no support, or such weak support, to their conclusions that it is reasonable to regard them as having a *flaw*. This may be because a mistake in logic is made in moving from the reasons to the conclusion, or it may be because the reasons support the conclusion only if they are accompanied by an implausible assumption. The skill of identifying flaws in reasoning is being able to see that the conclusion does not follow from the reasons or evidence, and being able to say *why* it does not follow. We illustrate this with the following examples.

Example 1: Violence on television

In Chapter 1, when discussing assumptions, we presented the following example of an argument:

> Some people say that the depiction of violence on television has no effect on viewers' behaviour. However, if what was shown on television did not affect behaviour, television advertising would never influence viewers to buy certain products. But we know that it does. So it cannot be true that television violence does not affect behaviour.

One way of summarising this piece of reasoning is:

> *Reason*: Television advertising affects viewers' behaviour.
>
> *Intermediate conclusion*: So, what is shown on television affects viewers' behaviour.
>
> *Main conclusion*: So, violence shown on television must affect viewers' behaviour.

If we take the intermediate conclusion as meaning that *some* of what is shown on television affects behaviour, then it does follow from the reason given, because television advertising *is* some of what is shown on television. However, the intermediate conclusion, interpreted in this way does not support the main conclusion, as it is intended to, because violence might be one of the things shown on television which does not affect behaviour. If, on the other hand we interpret the intermediate conclusion as meaning that *everything* shown on television affects behaviour, then it does not follow from the reason, because from the fact that one thing shown on television affects behaviour, it does not follow that everything else shown on television will do the same. So, whichever way we interpret the intermediate conclusion, this is not a good piece of reasoning, because it does not give good grounds for the conclusion it draws.

If we are asked to say what the flaw in the reasoning is, we could express it as follows:

The fact that *some things* which are shown on television affect viewers' behaviour is not a good reason for thinking that violence shown on television must affect viewers' behaviour,

or

The fact that *advertising* shown on television affects viewers' behaviour is not a good reason for accepting that *everything* shown on television affects viewers' behaviour.

The ability to state flaws in this way is an important skill to develop, because it can be an effective way of showing other people that there is something wrong with their reasoning. Note that we have stated this flaw without ever considering whether the basic reason – that television advertising affects viewers' behaviour – is true. If we can identify flaws in reasoning, then we can often be satisfied that a particular piece of reasoning does not establish its conclusion, without needing to dispute the truth of the claims upon which the conclusion is based.

We noted in our earlier discussion of the above example that another way of interpreting the argument was to see it as assuming, unjustifiably, that television advertising and violence shown on television were comparable, or analogous, in all relevant or important respects. When assessing arguments, it is useful to look out for analogies or comparisons, and to consider whether the two things which are being compared really are alike in ways which are relevant to the conclusion which is being drawn. This was evident in our discussion on pp. 47–8 of the argument about written tests for learner drivers in Portugal and the UK.

Example 2 : Affluence and health

Let us consider another example:

If people became healthier as the affluence of the country increased, we would expect the population to be healthier now than it was thirty years ago. But over the last thirty years new illnesses, such as chronic fatigue syndrome, have appeared, and we have become more vulnerable to old diseases such as heart disease, strokes and cancer. So the increased wealth of the country has not produced improvements in the health of the population.

The first thing to do when we want to assess whether an argument is flawed is to sort out what the conclusion is, and what evidence or reasons are offered for it. Before reading on, identify the conclusion and the reasons in this passage.

The conclusion, signalled by the word 'So' which introduces the last sentence, is:

> the increased wealth of the country has not produced improvements in the health of the population.

The evidence offered for this is that over a period during which the wealth of the country has increased, new diseases have appeared, and certain old diseases have become more common. Here is a more detailed analysis of the reasoning. There are two strands. First:

> *Basic Reason 1*: Over the last thirty years new illnesses, such as chronic fatigue syndrome, have appeared, and we have become more vulnerable to old diseases such as heart disease, strokes and cancer

This is intended to support an unstated:

> *Intermediate conclusion*: There have been no improvements in the health of the population over the last thirty years.

The second strand is as follows:

> *Assumption* (unstated): The affluence of the country has increased over the last thirty years.

This gives support to:

> *Basic Reason 2*: If people became healthier as the affluence of the country increased, we would expect the population to be healthier now than it was thirty years ago.

The intermediate conclusion and basic Reason 2 are then taken together to support the main conclusion. Before reading on, ask yourself whether any of the moves in this reasoning are flawed. Do you accept that the intermediate conclusion follows from basic Reason 1, that basic Reason 2 follows from the unstated assumption, and that the main conclusion follows from the intermediate conclusion together with basic Reason 2?

Remember that when we are looking for flaws, we are not considering whether the reasons are true. So, we do not ask, 'Is it true that the wealth of the country has increased over the last thirty years?' and 'Is it true that new diseases have appeared, and certain old ones have become more common?'. We say instead, 'Even if these claims are true, *do they give adequate support* to the conclusion that the increased wealth of the country has not produced improvements in the health of the population?' It is clear that they do not give adequate support, because we have not been given much information about the general health of the population. It may be true that there is more vulnerability to heart disease, strokes and cancer, but perhaps some 'old' diseases, for example tuberculosis and bronchitis, are much less common. Perhaps people have longer lives than was the case thirty years ago, and perhaps they are relatively healthy for long periods of their lives, before succumbing in old age to heart disease, strokes or cancer. There is a problem of interpretation here – what exactly is meant by 'the health of the population'? If we assume that it refers to the percentage of people's lives during which they are free from illness, then we have insufficient information upon which to base the conclusion.

Now we must state concisely what the flaw is:

> Even if some new diseases have appeared and some old diseases have become more common during the last thirty years, it does not follow that the population is less healthy than it was thirty years ago, because people may have long periods of good health before suffering from these diseases.

Note that the flaw occurs in the move from basic Reason 1 (the claim about prevalence of diseases) to the unstated intermediate conclusion (that the population is less healthy now than thirty years ago). Note also that, in establishing that this is a flawed argument, we have *not* established that the main conclusion is false. It may be true that the increased affluence of the country has not produced improvements in the health of the population. This could be true if, as the argument tries to suggest, there have been no improvements in the health of the population. But it could be true even if there have been improvements in the health of the population, because those improvements might have occurred even if the country had not become more affluent. So someone aiming to counter the original conclusion in the way set out in Example 3 would also be producing a flawed argument.

Example 3: Affluence and health – a connection

Making a connection between health and affluence, someone might reason:

> There have been improvements in the health of the population over the past thirty years, a period during which there has been an increase in the

affluence of the country. So the increased affluence of the country has produced the improvements in the health of the population.

The question as to whether increased affluence has or has not produced improvements in the health of the population cannot be settled without more evidence – evidence both about the incidence of all illnesses in the population, and about whether any improvements could not have occurred if there had not been greater affluence. The argument simply assumes, without producing any evidence for it, that because two things have occurred together, one of them must have caused the other.

This unwarranted assumption of a causal connection often occurs when someone discovers a correlation – that is, a connection between x and y such that whenever you find x, you are likely to find y, or such that whenever a person or a population has characteristic x, they are likely to have characteristic y. For example, suppose you find that children who frequently watch violent videos are likely to be aggressive; this may be because watching violent videos causes children to be aggressive, or it may be because having a natural tendency to aggressive behaviour causes children to enjoy watching violent videos. Or suppose you find that people who have a great deal of tooth decay are likely to be overweight. This may be because a third factor – perhaps eating large amounts of sugary foods – causes both these conditions. All that you have found when you have discovered a correlation is that two things occur together. This may be because x causes y, or because y causes x, or because x and y are both caused by something else, or it may be simply coincidence . You are guilty of flawed reasoning if you just assume, without further evidence that x causes y.

Nevertheless it is important to note that discovering correlations is *not* a pointless exercise. It is often the first step in the attempt to investigate whether there is a causal connection between two phenomena.

Example 4: Exhaustion of mineral resources

Here is our last example in this section.

It has always been the case in the past that new discoveries of mineral resources have kept pace with demand. For example, bauxite reserves have tripled in the last ten years, while demand has doubled over the same period. At no time have the known reserves of minerals been as great as the total mineral resources of the world. Therefore, even though at any given time we know of only a limited supply of any mineral, we can be confident that there is no imminent danger of our running out of mineral resources.

Before reading on, identify the conclusion and the reasons in this argument, and try to state for yourself what is going wrong in moving from the reasons to the conclusion.

The main conclusion, clearly signalled by 'Therefore', is the final sentence. The argument can be regarded as having the following structure:

Reason 1: It has always been the case in the past that new discoveries of mineral reserves have kept pace with demand.

Reason 2: At no time have the known reserves of minerals been as great as the total mineral resources of the world.

These two reasons, taken together, are intended to support:

Main conclusion: Therefore, even though at any given time we know of only a limited supply of any mineral, we can be confident that there is no imminent danger of our running out of mineral resources.

Note that the example presented in the second sentence is being used to give some support to Reason 1. But we have not shown this as a reason from which Reason 1 follows, because one example could not be sufficient to establish a general claim such as Reason 1, nor is it likely that the author of the argument thinks that the example does establish the general claim. It is being used in an illustrative way. The second sentence *could* be included in the argument structure by simply treating it as a part of Reason 1.

Since this argument is clearly relying on past experience, it may be tempting to describe the flaw as an assumption that what has been true in the past will continue to be true in the future. But this assumption under-lies many arguments, particularly those relying on laws of science (for example that at sea level, water boils at 100 degrees Celsius), and in many such contexts, it is not an unreasonable assumption to make.

So we need to state the flaw more specifically. Why should we *not* conclude that there is no imminent danger of running out of mineral resources, based on evidence that at any given time in the past the known reserves of minerals have not been as great as the total mineral resources of the world? It is reasonable to assume that the mineral resources of the world are finite, and thus that if they continue to be used they will run out at some time in the future, and we cannot know when that point will be reached. We can state the flaw as follows:

Assuming that the mineral resources of the world are finite, at present (and at any given time in the future) the total mineral resources of the world may be no greater than the known reserves of minerals.

A further point could be made about this argument. It makes no mention of evidence which may be relevant – i.e. a possible acceleration in the rate at which mineral resources are being used.

Some ways in which arguments can be flawed

We have now seen five different ways in which an argument can be flawed. In Example 1, on the effects of television violence, one interpretation of the argument was flawed because *it drew a general conclusion* about the effects of television *from just one case* (advertising) of which the effects were claimed to be known. The flaw in the other interpretation of the argument was that *it relied on an inappropriate analogy* or comparison. In Example 2, the original argument about increased affluence and health, the argument was flawed because *it drew its conclusion on the basis of insufficient evidence* (the evidence that *some* old diseases are more prevalent), whilst at the same time *failing to look for other relevant evidence* (for example, the reduced incidence of some diseases, the percentage of people's lives during which they are free of illness, and so on). In Example 3, claiming that increased affluence had produced an improvement in the health of the population, the argument was flawed because *it assumed that because two things have occurred together, one has caused the other*, and because *it failed to consider other possible causes* of the improvements in the health of the population. In Example 4 the argument concluded that exhaustion of the mineral resources of the world was not imminent. It was flawed because *it disregarded relevant factors* (the finite nature of mineral resources, and the rate of use of mineral resources).

There are some flaws which appear quite often in reasoning, and which can deceive the reader into thinking that good reasoning has been presented. This is true of the flaw in Example 1 above – drawing a general conclusion from just one example – and of the flaw in Example 3 – assuming a causal connection on the basis of an association between two things. These are two instances of faults which are generally called 'fallacies', and some texts begin their discussion of faults in reasoning with a list of fallacies. In this text we have started with a different approach, which requires engaging with the particular subject matter of each argument. The skill which needs to be developed is an ability to say what is going wrong in the move from the reasons to the conclusion *in a particular argument*.

There are two reasons why we should not rely simply on lists of fallacies when trying to identify flaws. The first is that arguments can be flawed in ways which do not appear in lists of fallacies – the flaw in Example 4 above is evidence of this. Second, relying simply on lists of fallacies can encourage us to overlook the context of the argument, and to classify arguments in a way which can cut off further reasoning instead of allowing us to engage with the topic in its own context.

An example can clarify our last point. A category which usually appears in lists of fallacies is the '*slippery-slope*' argument. This refers to reasoning in which it is claimed that a certain action, or the introduction of a certain policy, though possibly harmless in itself, will be the first step along a road to inevitable and undesirable consequences. For example, someone may argue that we should not legalise the sale and use of cannabis because to do so would set us upon a slippery slope to legalisation of more harmful drugs. A satisfactory criticism of this argument would require more than saying: 'slippery-slope argument, therefore flawed'. It would require us to say why *in this particular case*, the supposed undesirable consequence need not occur. This is a much more challenging task, because the introduction of legislation *can* act as a precedent in some circumstances, and *can* change the climate of opinion in such a way as to make some further consequence more likely to happen.

However, being aware of some standard fallacies may help you to see in some cases what is going wrong in an argument, so we mention a few more here.

The *ad hominem* fallacy occurs when someone attempts to discredit another's argument by mentioning disreputable aspects of the person's character, instead of focusing on what is wrong with the argument itself. Establishing, for example, that someone is a bully is not a good reason to conclude that their reasoning must be at fault. As we indicated in the section on reliability of authorities, *some* personal characteristics (for example, a tendency to exaggerate, or a temporary or permanent mental incapacity) may be relevant to judgements about the reliability of *information* which others give us. But it is fallacious to claim that a particular conclusion does not follow from acceptable evidence or true reasons, simply on the grounds that the person drawing the conclusion has an unpleasant personality.

One fallacious type of argument involves confusing *necessary and sufficient conditions*. Here are two examples in which this occurs. See if you can state exactly what is going wrong in each case:

> You can't win a five set tennis match if you are unfit. But you are fitter than your opponent, so you will win.

> You will be rich if you win the lottery. But you never buy a lottery ticket, so you will never be rich.

In the first example the flaw is that it assumes that because it is *necessary* to be fit in order to win a five set tennis match, being the fitter player is *sufficient* to guarantee a win. But this assumption is ill-founded, because winning a tennis match depends on skill as well as fitness. The second argument is flawed because it wrongly assumes that something which is *sufficient* to guarantee riches – winning the lottery – is *necessary* in order to become rich.

Someone is said to commit the *straw man fallacy* if their argument relies on misrepresenting the opponent's point of view. In January 2001, an injunction was granted preventing publication of information as to the whereabouts of the killers of a child, James Bulger. The judge, Dame Elizabeth Butler-Sloss, gave her reasons for the judgment – that if, after their release from custody, the whereabouts of these two young men became public knowledge they would be seriously at risk of death or injury, and that the European Convention on Human Rights – now part of UK law through the Human Rights Act of 1998 – obliges the state to protect an individual's right to life. Suppose someone objected to the judgment on the grounds that it is based on the view that the killers should be rewarded for becoming reformed characters during their period of detention. This would be setting up a *straw man*, that is, an argument which can easily be knocked down because it is obviously weak, but which is not what the proponent of the original argument believes or claims.

The fallacy of *begging the question* involves taking for granted that which one was claiming to conclude, as illustrated in the following argument:

> We know that Jesus was the son of God, because he said so, and the son of God would not lie.

The conclusion that Jesus was the son of God does not follow from the two reasons offered – that he said so, and that the son of God would not lie – without the assumption that the person who said he was the son of God was indeed the son of God, that is without taking for granted the truth of what it aimed to prove.

We have shown some of the ways in which arguments can be flawed. In order to become skilled in identifying flaws in arguments, it is helpful to practise on numerous arguments on a wide range of subject matter. Using lists of fallacies may help you to begin to say what is wrong with an argument, but remember that arguments can go wrong in ways which do not fit neatly into these categories. We have pointed out that this was true of Example 4 above, about the world reserves of mineral resources, in which the flaw could be stated only by referring to the particular subject matter of the argument. For the next exercise, remember that you are to focus simply on the skill of identifying flaws – you should not worry in this exercise about whether the reasons are true. Bear in mind the following points:

1 Identify the main conclusion.
2 Identify the reasons and the way in which they are meant to support the main conclusion.
3 For each step of the argument, ask 'Does this (main or intermediate) conclusion follow from the reasons which are given for it'?
4 Explain why the conclusion does not follow – i.e. think of a reason why the conclusion *might* not be true, even if the reason(s) are true, and try to do this by referring to the subject matter of the argument, and not merely stating the name of a fallacy.

Exercise 9: Identifying flaws

Identify the flaws in the following pieces of reasoning:

1 A fantastic basketball team could be created if the best player from each of the best teams formed a new club. Basketball would then become an exciting game for fans everywhere.
   (Law School Admission Test, October 1985)

2 Crimes and outrages of all sorts have been committed under a full moon by a wide variety of people. The advice to derive from this is clear: when the moon is full, trust no-one, not even yourself.
   (Law School Admission Test, September 1984)

3 Young people today have more formal education than their grandparents had. Wilma is young, so she must have more formal education than her grandparents had.
   (Law School Admission Test, 1982)

4 Neither marijuana nor LSD can be harmful, since they are used by doctors to ease the pain of cancer patients.
   (Law School Admission Test, 1982)

5 Adolescents frequently suffer from anaemia, but this is not, as is often supposed, due to insufficient iron in their diets, but is a result of this group's having a higher requirement for iron than that of the rest of the population.
   (Law School Admission Test, February 1983)

---

6   We know that diet is an important cause of disease. One example of a disease which is attributable to diet is the heart attack, which is so common in Western countries. In countries with different diets, the diseases differ also. For example, in Japan the most common fatal diseases are strokes and cancers of the stomach. The Japanese diet has a much lower fat content and a much higher fibre content than the Western diet. So if people in the West were to adopt a Japanese low-fat/high fibre diet, they would be unlikely to die from heart attacks. They would die instead from the diseases which are common in Japan – that is to say, strokes and cancers of the stomach.

7   Who invented cooking? Since cooking requires heat, the first cooks must have used fire. Until recently, there was no evidence of fire having been used earlier than 200,000 years ago. But now, reliable scientific evidence has shown that the ancestors of *Homo sapiens* were lighting fires almost 400,000 years ago. So cooking must have been invented at that time.

8   The witness said that he had seen Fred in the vicinity of the shop at the time the fire was started. But we know this witness has a grudge against Fred, and he has been known to give unreliable evidence in the past. So we cannot rely on this person's statement. Hence Fred must have been somewhere else when the fire was started.

9   Most people could be musical geniuses if they practised hard enough. A psychologist interested in whether genius is mainly hard work rather than inspiration has examined the lives of seventy-six composers. Most of them had at least a decade of painstaking training before they wrote any masterpieces. Mozart, for example, was drilled incessantly by his father in techniques of composition before he composed his first work of genius at the age of 12.

10   Some people claim that poverty is one of the causes of crime. But there can't be any kind of link between being poor and committing crimes, because lots of people who are poor never commit a crime.

Answers to Exercise 9 are given on pp. 159–61.

Evaluating further evidence

Often when we present a case to someone else for accepting a particular conclusion, they will say, 'Ah, but what about . . .?', offering some piece of information which we have not mentioned and which they think weakens our case. In relation to our earlier example concerning the dangers of smoking, imagine someone saying to you, 'Knowing that smoking is dangerous cannot be sufficient to stop people from smoking, because there has been so much publicity about the health risks, and yet people still smoke'. Let us suppose that a survey of smokers' beliefs has been carried out. You might then reply to the above statement, 'Ah, but what about that survey which showed that, unlike non-smokers, smokers generally believe that smoking is *not* bad for one's health?' The other person must then consider what impact this has on their conclusion.

Being able to assess the impact of additional evidence is valuable because people frequently challenge each other's reasoning by offering some new piece of information. One response to such challenges would be to question the truth of the new piece of evidence, and this would involve one of the skills we have already mentioned – that of evaluating the truth of evidence or reasons. Another response might be to say that even if the new piece of evidence were true, it would not weaken the conclusion. This involves the other vital skill which we have discussed – that of assessing the degree of support which a reason gives to a conclusion.

Of course, the context may not be one in which we are trying to defend a conclusion – nor should we be thinking in terms of the necessity to defend a conclusion at all costs. That would be to indulge in uncritical thinking – being determined to believe something even in the face of evidence to the contrary. So we must be prepared to acknowledge that sometimes additional evidence will weaken our conclusions. Sometimes new evidence comes to light not in the context of a discussion, not when someone else is trying to undermine one's own reasoning, but simply in relation to a subject upon which we already hold an opinion, and believe that we hold that opinion for good reasons. Once we see that the new evidence is relevant to the issue, we must then consider whether it counts for or against our earlier opinion – that is to say we must consider whether it *strengthens* our reasoning and not merely whether it *weakens* it.

Exercise 10: Evaluating further evidence

This exercise gives you practice in evaluating the impact of additional evidence on an argument. For each of the following multiple choice questions, pick the correct response, explain why it is the correct response, and explain why each of the other responses is incorrect.

1   A recent study found that school-age children who participate in school-related sports activities fight less during school and school-related activities than do those children who do not participate. It was concluded that sports must satisfy an aggressive impulse which would otherwise be released through fighting.

Which of the following, if true, weakens the conclusion referred to in the above passage?

(a)   School-related sports activities are always supervised by adults.

(b)   Supervisors of school-related sports activities discourage participants from being extremely aggressive.

(c)   Children who participate in school-related sports activities tend to be more aggressive physically than those who do not participate.

(d)   Approximately 85 per cent of the fights children get into during school or school-related activities take place during break times.

(e)   Most schools suspend those who fight during school or school-related activities from the schools' sports teams.

(Law School Admission Test, 1982)

2   Although the number of undergraduates studying engineering has grown greatly over the last five years, there may be a shortage of engineering teachers in the near future because the number of people receiving PhDs in engineering, those most likely to teach, has not been increasing. This results because the high salaries offered to engineers without advanced degrees reduce the incentive to pursue post-graduate studies. Therefore, businesses will have to recognise that their long-term interests would best be served by reducing salaries for those without advanced degrees.

Which of the following, if true, would *most* weaken the above argument?

(a) Enrolment in the sciences has grown over the last five years.

(b) Fewer than half of the people who have received PhDs in engineering teach full-time.

(c) Businesses pay high salaries to engineers with advanced degrees.

(d) The increases in engineering enrolment are due to the high salaries paid by businesses.

(e) Many university programmes are funded by businesses interested in engineering research.

(Law School Admission Test, December 1983)

3 *Joan*: One method of reducing serious crime in the United States is to adopt the English system of providing free heroin to heroin addicts.

Anna: That's absurd. It's just like giving free cars to automobile thieves.

Which of the following, if true, would *most* strengthen Joan's argument?

(a) Heroin addicts are more likely to be violent under the influence of drugs than when they are anticipating using those drugs.

(b) The amount of money needed annually to supply heroin to heroin addicts is less than the amount lost annually by the victims of drug-related crimes.

(c) It is cheaper to provide addicts with drugs than to jail them after they have committed crimes.

(d) The amount of serious crime committed by non-addicts is roughly equal in England and the US.

(e) A substantial amount of serious crime is committed by heroin addicts in order to support their habits.

(Law School Admission Test, October 1983)

4 Since only 4 per cent of all automobiles fail the state's annual safety inspection solely because of defective direction indicators, the state's automobile association recommends that direction indicators no longer be inspected. Although they are an important safety feature, too few are defective to make the expense of testing them worthwhile.

Which of the following, if true, points out the *most* serious weakness in the recommendations of the automobile association?

(a) Owners will no longer maintain their automobile direction indicators in working order if the inspection requirement is dropped.

(b) Owners of automobiles with defective direction indicators may not have learned to use manual direction signals.

(c) Eliminating the inspection of the direction indicators will make the state's inspection procedure less thorough than those of neighbouring states.

(d) Automobiles with defective direction indicators will fail inspection anyway if they have other safety defects.

(e) Automobiles that have defective direction indicators may have other defects not covered by the safety inspection system.

(Law School Admission Test, February 1983)

5   A recent study found that if children watched up to one hour of television a day, their performance in school was unaffected, but if they watched between two and three hours a day, they were likely to perform considerably less well than their peers who watched less. The researchers concluded that if parents carefully monitored the time their children watched television, the children's school performance would be maintained at adequate levels.

If true, which of the following statements about the children in the study would *most* strengthen the conclusions of the researchers?

(a) Most of the children who performed at below-average levels in school watched more than two hours of television a day.

(b) Children who watched television mostly at weekends performed better in school than children who watched television mostly on school nights.

(c) Children who spent more time reading than watching television performed better in school than those who did not.

(d) The disparities among the children in terms of school performance lessened when the television viewing habits of the children became more uniform.

(e) The children who reduced the amount of television they watched daily spent the extra time reading.

(Law School Admission Test, December 1985)

6   It is unwise to continue the career training and employment pro-
     grammes administered in most prisons today. These programmes do
     not achieve what they are meant to achieve because most ex-pris-
     oners choose not to pursue the occupations they followed during the
     time they spent in prison.

     Which of the following, if true, *most* weakens the above argument?

     (a)   Many habits and skills learnt in prison training programmes
            are valuable in a great variety of occupations.

     (b)   Prisons have an obligation to provide prisoners with occupa-
            tional training they will later use in employment.

     (c)   Prison career training programmes tend to make prisoners
            more productive during their time in prison.

     (d)   Training prisoners for future employment is a major goal of
            most rehabilitation programmes today.

     (e)   In most prisons today, prisoners can prepare for their choice
            of a number of occupations.

                                        (Law School Admission Test, 1986)

7   Certain physiological changes accompany the psychological stress of
     telling a lie. Reliable lie detection is possible, because, with the
     appropriate instruments, we can measure the physiological symp-
     toms of lying.

     Which of the following, if true, *most* weakens the above argument?

     (a)   Lie detectors are expensive machines, and they require careful
            maintenance.

     (b)   Some people find lying only moderately stress-inducing.

     (c)   Lie detection requires highly trained, capable personnel.

     (d)   Even the appropriate instrument can be misused and abused.

     (e)   Numerous kinds of psychological stress produce similar physio-
            logical symptoms.

                                  (Law School Admission Test, March 1984)

Answers to Exercise 10 are given on pp. 162–6.

Questioning explanations

Some pieces of reasoning, rather than trying to convince us that we should accept a particular conclusion, aim instead to *explain* something which we already accept as being true. This is a case of giving *reasons why* something is as it is, rather than giving *reasons for* believing something. The difference is illustrated by the following report from *The Independent* of 17 February 1994.

> Latest figures for cancers in England and Wales show an increase of 4 per cent in 1988. Richard Doll, consultant to the Imperial Cancer Research Fund, said one explanation was the rising number of elderly people.

Richard Doll's comments are not trying to convince us of the fact that cancers increased in 1988. They are taking the truth of that for granted, and trying to explain why this increase occurred.

This is a case of an explanation occurring as an independent piece of reasoning, but we may also find explanations offered within an argument, as part of a longer passage of reasoning. What we need to know about an explanation is whether it is the correct explanation. It may not be easy to settle such a question, but there are strategies we can use to attempt to make some assessment of an explanation. One is to examine any questionable assumptions underlying the explanation. Another is to think of possible alternative explanations, and try to find further evidence which may rule out some of these explanations. If we can think of two or three equally plausible explanations of something, then we should be cautious about accepting any of them as the correct explanation until we have further information.

We can try these strategies on the above example, although it may seem presumptuous to question the judgement of a leading authority in cancer research! What assumptions underlie Richard Doll's explanation? If the increase in cancers is attributable to 'rising numbers of elderly people', this must be because people who, had they lived in earlier times, would have died from other diseases (which are now more easily treatable or preventable) are living to an age at which they are likely to get cancer. No doubt further support for this assumption could be found by examining figures on the incidence of cancer in different age groups.

What alternative explanations of the increase in cancer can we suggest? Well, there would be an increase in cancer figures if the population in general were more susceptible to the disease – perhaps because of pollutants in the environment. There would be an increase in the figures if particular groups had a greater incidence of cancer, due to changes in habits and practices. For example, it could be that new medications for circulatory diseases cause more cancers, or that more cancers are caused by more women taking hormone replacement therapy. Light could be shed on the plausibility of these alternative explanations by examining figures on the incidence of cancer amongst different groups. We are not suggesting that Richard Doll's explanation is likely to be incorrect – in fact he is more than likely to have taken all these factors into account before offering his explanation. But the example serves to illustrate the way in which we can question explanations, perhaps reserve judgement on them until we have more information, and perhaps take steps to investigate which of various alternative explanations is the most plausible.

The following passage describes a piece of research which aimed to find out the most plausible explanation of a known fact. It is adapted from an article in *The Independent on Sunday*, 25 June 1995.

Motorists in their teens and twenties have a low opinion of elderly drivers, whom they regard as bumbling old fools who shouldn't be allowed on the roads.

Some old drivers are indeed incompetent, and data from the US has shown that the accident rate for drivers rises substantially after the age of 70. A research team at the University of California at Los Angeles has now carried out a detailed study of the abilities of elderly drivers.

The research team recruited volunteers in their early seventies who, according to their doctors, had signs of early dementia due to Alzheimer's disease, or to narrowing of the arteries. Other drivers of the same age had diabetes as their only medical condition, and a group of younger drivers was used for comparison.

All the drivers – the demented, the diabetics and the young controls – were taken on a drive around a three-mile road network with intersections, speed bumps, traffic signs, signals and parking lots. Each driver's performance was graded by an instructor in the car, which was fitted with an on-board computer which recorded braking speed, steering, crossing the centre line, and so on. The drivers also worked their way through a series of standard tests of mental ability, concentration and short-term memory.

The results showed that the 70-year-olds with diabetes did just as well on the test drives and mental tests as the younger drivers. The drivers with early dementia did worse. They drove slowly, and the mistakes they made were serious – for example, turning into a one-way street marked 'no entry'.

The conclusion was that drivers in their 70s in normal health (with normal vision) can perform at a level comparable with young, healthy adults – at least in a suburban, non-stressing environment. Statistics showing that drivers in this age group have high accident rates are, the report says, at least partly attributable to people continuing to drive after they have become mildly demented.

('Second opinion', Dr Tony Smith,
The Independent on Sunday, 25 June 1995)

Before reading on, ask yourself the following questions:

- What was the known fact which the study sought to explain?
- What explanation would the author expect young motorists to give?
- what explanation does the report of the study give?

The passage tells us in the second paragraph that data from the US shows that the accident rate for drivers rises substantially after the age of 70. This is the fact which is to be explained, and it means, of course, that *as a group* the drivers aged over 70 have a higher percentage of accidents than those aged under 70. It is clear from the first paragraph that the author would expect young drivers to explain this fact by saying that *all* drivers aged over 70 are incompetent, and therefore more likely to have accidents. The study did tests to assess the competence of drivers, and found that those aged over 70 who had dementia were less competent than young drivers, but those aged over 70 who did not have this medical condition were no less competent than young drivers.

This suggests that the most plausible explanation of the higher accident rate amongst drivers aged over 70 is that *some* drivers aged over 70 are incompetent due to dementia. We should note that the article suggests that the driving test was conducted in a 'suburban, non-stressing environment'. If this is correct, then, in order to be certain that the explanation offered by the study was the most plausible, we would want some evidence about the competence of both young drivers and drivers aged over 70 in more stressful traffic conditions.

The report does not make clear the age range of the 'young control' group. Dividing all drivers into only two groups, over 70 and under 70, obscures any statistical differences in the very large under-70 group. This is an example of how critical of statistics we must be, even when we accept them. For example, drivers aged under 25 have a significantly higher accident rate than those over 25. Elderly drivers might wish to argue that this showed a high incidence of undiagnosed dementia among younger drivers!

Exercise 11: Offering alternative explanations

For each of the following passages, identify which part of the passage is the explanation, and which part is the fact which is being explained. Then suggest an alternative explanation for this fact. Do not worry if you are uncertain whether your explanation is true. Just try to think of something which, if it were true, would be another possible explanation:

1   Public confidence in the police force is declining at the same time as fear of crime is growing. People's lack of confidence in the police is the reason why they are so much more fearful of crime.

2   Why has the divorce rate increased so much over the last thirty years? It is because there are so many more couples these days who are unhappily married.

3   The human race has never received a well-authenticated communication from beings elsewhere in the universe. This is because the only intelligent life in the universe is on our own planet.

4   The number of cars per head of population in Britain continues to rise. This is why, whenever a new road such as the M25 is built, the density of traffic in that area increases.

5   Because the weather was so bad in Britain last summer, the number of people taking holidays in British resorts declined.

Answers to Exercise 11 are given on pp. 166–7.

Exercise 12: Identifying and evaluating explanations

In each of the following three passages, an explanation is offered, or various different explanations are considered, for a given fact or phenomenon. For each passage:

   (a)   identify the fact or phenomenon which is to be explained;

   (b)   find the explanation or explanations given in the passage;

(c) think of any other possible explanations which are not mentioned in the passage; and

(d) either

- say which explanation you think is the most plausible, and why; or

- think about further evidence you would need in order to decide which explanation is the most plausible.

This exercise could form the basis of a class discussion.

1 Girls doing well while boys feel neglected, study finds

'Boys are blamed for everything', complained a 14-year-old, encapsulating the jaundiced view of school that seems to be having such a bad effect on boys' exam results.

'It was a myth that girls perform poorly at school', said Michael Younger, whose study of an East Anglian comprehensive elicited the 14-year-old boy's comment. Boys are the problem.

The boy also complained: 'Girls are treated a lot better and get first choice of equipment and task.'

Reflecting the national picture, the girls at this school have done consistently better at GCSE than the boys, although the gap has narrowed.

Mr Younger said some schools should take credit for implementing equal opportunities policies which had reduced discrimination against girls. They now had to tackle boys' under-achievement and disengagement, although Mr Younger admitted that it was a complex problem to which he did not have any easy answers.

He and Molly Warrington, his fellow researcher at Homerton College, Cambridge, found that boys felt they were unfairly treated or neglected in class, although teachers and the majority of girls disagreed.

Staff said boys went to considerable lengths not to appear swotty – for instance, denying to classmates they had done homework even when they had, or playing up in class. They saw boys as unable to concentrate or organise themselves and lacking in motivation.

Girls tended to be more focused, and study was not seen as bad for their image. Parents and teachers agreed that girls did more homework, while boys saw it as a necessary evil to be done as quickly as possible.

Seventy per cent of girls thought female teachers treated boys and girls equally; only 46 per cent of boys agreed.

A majority of all the pupils surveyed thought male teachers were biased towards girls, however – accepting behaviour from girls which they punished in boys.

A fifth form girl agreed that girls were treated more leniently by male teachers. 'The girls have a reputation for being well-behaved, so if, for example, they don't do their homework they won't get told off as much.'

Boys from the same year complained that they got less attention from male teachers than the girls did.

Girls appeared to have clearer goals, said Mr Younger, which led them to focus on their work. Some boys had no idea what they wanted to do after GCSE and several had no idea what later courses to take.

(© *The Guardian*, 26 August 1995)

2 Number of road deaths at post-war record low

Fewer people were killed on Britain's roads last year than in any year since 1926, but a rise in the number of those seriously injured suggests that further improvements are unlikely.

Preliminary figures released by the Department of Transport suggest that 3,651 people died on the roads, a fall of 4 per cent compared with 1993 when 3,814 died – the previous post-war record low.

The fall in deaths, despite an increase in road traffic of 3 per cent, appears to be explained by better paramedic treatment at the roadside and improved medical care, since the figures for serious injuries have increased to 46,784, a rise of 4 per cent.

In fact the number of deaths is just about the only figure to have gone down between 1993 and 1994. Serious injuries for both car users and pedestrians also increased. Indeed pedestrian casualties rose by 2 per cent overall from 1993 levels to 49,026 and while deaths fell by 7 per cent to 1,148, serious injuries increased by 4 per cent to 11,924.

While Britain generally has a good safety record on the roads compared with its European neighbours, the number of child casualties is proportionally higher and last year reinforced the trend, with child casualties going up by 6 per cent to 45,239. The number of child pedestrians killed on the road went up from 135 to 173, a rise of 28 per cent.

The increase in injuries means that the Government has virtually no chance of meeting its target of reducing total roads casualties by one-third between the early Eighties and 2000. However, it will easily achieve the target on deaths if present trends continue.

Edmund King, campaigns manager of the RAC, said: 'There are very worrying features about these figures, particularly on child deaths. One thing that could be done quite easily is to bring the clocks into line with the Continent so that children would not have to go home from school in the dark.'

He says that the increase in serious injuries shows that the number of accidents is rising and he feels many are caused by drivers feeling too insulated in their modern cars. Mr King said; 'They listen to the stereo, have the heater on and it's almost as if the outside world doesn't exist. And then they fall asleep or make a mistake . . .'

Brigitte Chaudhry, national secretary of RoadPeace, an organisation for road accident victims, said the figures on deaths may be misleading; 'Deaths are only counted as such if they occur within 30 days of the accident. Nowadays, many people are kept alive for much longer thanks to modern medical techniques and die later than that.'

She added that the main reason for the reduction in deaths over the last 30 years is a decline in the number of vulnerable road users, such as pedestrians and cyclists, using the roads: 'As there are fewer pedestrians on the road and more are getting hurt, it suggests that roads are more dangerous and not safer.'

(*The Independent*, 31 March 1995)

3 Science debunks miracle of weeping madonna

The only weeping madonna officially accepted by the Roman Catholic Church has been exposed as a fake by an Italian scientist who used the logic of Mr Spock, the deductive reasoning of Sherlock Holmes and a knowledge of capillary attraction.

There has been a sharp increase in the sightings of weeping madonnas, from Ireland to Croatia, but the only one recognised by the Church is a statue of the Virgin Mary in the town of Siracusa in Sicily. It first began weeping in 1953.

The 'miracle' of a statue that appears to weep has even been caught on film. But Luigi Garlaschelli, a chemistry researcher at the University of Pavia, believes he has an explanation.

Dr Garlaschelli has made his own weeping madonna which baffled onlookers into believing the statue was able to shed tears without any mechanical or electronic aids or the deployment of water-absorbing chemicals.

The secret, he revealed, is to use a hollow statue made of thin plaster. If it is coated with an impermeable glazing and water poured into the hollow centre from a tiny hole in the head, the statue behaves quite normally.

The plaster absorbs the liquid but the glazing prevents it from pouring out. But if barely perceptible scratches are made in the glazing over the eyes, droplets of water appear as if by divine intervention – rather than by capillary attraction, the movement of water through sponge-like material.

Dr Garlaschelli said: 'I notice that, among these weeping madonna miracles, the only one accepted by the Catholic Church happened in Siracusa in 1953. This is the best documented case, with many witnesses to an actual case of weeping, and even a couple of amateur films showing watery tears appearing on the face out of the blue.

'Examination of a copy of this bas-relief from the same manufacturer as the original, however, proved it to be made of glazed plaster and to possess a cavity behind the face.'

Dr Garlaschelli said the actual madonna of Siracusa is kept behind a glass partition and he is unable to inspect its glazing for himself. 'I think permission won't be granted to examine it,' he said. 'Many of these relics are not allowed to be examined.'

(*The Independent on Sunday*, 9 July 1995)

Answers to Exercise 12 are given on pp. 167–8.

Summarising the skills of evaluation

The skills discussed in this chapter need to be used together when assessing a passage of reasoning. We need to consider whether the reasons, and any unstated assumptions, are true; whether the argument relies upon evidence from anyone whose authority is questionable; whether anything which we ourselves know, but which is not stated in the passage, weakens or strengthens the conclusion; whether, if the passage relies upon an explanation, we can think of equally plausible alternative explanations; and finally whether we can identify flaws in the reasoning which show us that the conclusion is not well supported by the reasons.

Here is a checklist to work through when assessing the reasoning in the passages in Exercise 13.

1 Find the conclusion.
2 Find the reasons and any unstated assumptions.
3 Consider how far you can go in assessing the truth of the reasons and the unstated assumptions. Think about how you would seek further information to enable you to assess the truth of reasons.
4 Does the reasoning rely on evidence from sources whose authority is questionable?
5 Do you yourself have any knowledge which strengthens or weakens the conclusion? (Remember to subject your own 'knowledge' to the same standards of scrutiny as you apply to the claims made by other people!)
6 Does the passage contain any explanations? If so, are they plausible, and are they the only plausible explanations of what is being explained?
7 If you believe that the conclusion is not well supported by the reasons and assumptions, can you state the way in which the move from reasons to conclusion is flawed?

Exercise 13: Practising the skills

Identify and evaluate the reasoning in each of the following passages.

1 Extract from 'Television – a force for good in our nation's prisons'

. . . it would be mad for Mr Straw [the Home Secretary] not to proceed with the proposal to unleash the BBC and commercial TV companies on the prison population. It is the right thing pragmatically and in principle too.

Why? First because of what British prisons are like. In the main, they are grossly overcrowded, very uncomfortable already and constant hives of crime-behind-bars. Men who are left with nothing to do, many of them being illiterate, currently amuse themselves with drugs, sex, constant little vendettas and a little light violence. Because of over-crowding, they spend more and more time in their cells. Is 'Have We Got News for You', or 'Casualty' or 'Brookside' really a worse alternative than cannabis and recreational buggery?

Furthermore, increasingly, television means communication with the rest of us, albeit one-way communication. For the modern citizen, TV is the ubiquitous window on society, a prime source of thinking and infor-mation. It shapes us. Now, granted, prisoners are physically cut off from society, but that is as much for our safety as for their punishment. Assuming that we hold to the idea of rehabilitation and the return of pris-oners to ordinary life after their sentences, then cutting them off from social trends, thinking, entertainment and news is pointless, even stupid. Prisoners who watch television for hours are not only likelier to be easier to guard and oversee; they are also likely to end up more like the rest of us.

The second reason we approve of television in jails is that inmates would not be given them free, but would have to pay for the privilege, using money earned inside jail. TVs would be removed for bad behaviour. Prison is such a bizarre and alienating environment that anything which keeps inmates in touch with ordinary life is useful; earning and paying is useful because it increases, however marginally, responsibility. It is what prisoners will quickly have to learn to do outside.

This is, in short, a proposal which is sensible in security terms, mildly rehabilitative and – yes – humane.

(David Aaronovitch, *The Independent*, 30 November 1997)

2   Extract from 'The economic case for drugs'

America spends at least $20 billion (£13 billion) year on drug enforce-ment, and arrests more than one million people a year on drug charges. Yet, according to standard economic analysis and existing evidence, drug legalisation would be a far superior policy to drug prohibition.

Drug prohibition does not eliminate drug markets or drug use; it simply moves them underground. Prohibition raises some costs of doing business for drug suppliers, and it probably reduces demand by some consumers.

But substantial drug consumption persists even in the most repres-sive prohibition regimes. Data in the US suggests that more than 30 per cent of the population aged 12 and over has used marijuana, and more than 10 per cent has used cocaine. Violation of prohibition is widespread.

Prohibition increases violence, because buyers and sellers of drugs cannot use the official justice system to resolve disputes. Prohibition also plays a key role in non-violent kinds of crime, by diverting criminal justice resources from the deterrence of non-drug crime. It facilitates the corruption of police, judges and politicians, partly because huge profits are at stake, partly because the legal channels of influence are not available.

The homicide rate rose rapidly in America after 1910, when many states adopted drug and alcohol prohibition laws, and it rose through World War I and during the 1920s as efforts to enforce alcohol prohibition increased, but then fell dramatically after Prohibition's repeal in 1934. In the late 1960s, homicide again increased dramatically and stayed at historically high levels throughout the 1970s and 1980s, coinciding with a drastic increase in drug law enforcement.

Prohibition also means diminished health. In a black market, the drug users face a heightened uncertainty concerning the quality and purity of the drugs they purchase, plus an incentive to consume drugs using methods, such as injection, that are unhealthy but give the biggest bang for the buck.

During alcohol Prohibition in the US, deaths due to alcoholism rose relative to other proxies for alcohol consumption, presumably because consumption of adulterated alcohol increased.

On top of these deleterious effects, using prohibition to deter drug consumption means society cannot levy taxes on sales of drugs or collect income taxes from those working in the drug trade. This means drug suppliers and drug users – persons deliberately breaking society's rules – gain at the expense of taxpayers generally.

(Jeffrey Miron, The Observer, 15 August 1999)

3 Extract from 'There are greater dangers to children than mobile phones'

Yesterday's report by the distinguished experts on the risk posed by mobile phones is a good review of the current state of knowledge, and its conclusion can be summed up as a large 'Don't know'. That is the kind of conclusion which modern society, with its lust for certainty, is bad at handling.

Their recommendation that the use of mobiles by children should be minimised errs on the side of caution, as it should. But then, a similar committee in the 1950s, if told that people would spend 25 hours a week in front of a cathode-ray tube, would probably have recommended that children should not watch 'inessential' television.

Only three effects of using mobiles have been proved. One is a slight heating of the brain. On that basis, we might as well prevent children from wearing hats.

The second is a speeding up of reaction times in robust, controlled experiments that compare random groups of people whose heads were subjected — or not — to the low levels of microwaves emitted by mobile phones. That is worrying, because it suggests that this kind of radiation has some biological effect. That warrants caution and further research.

The third is an increased chance of death or injury from using a mobile while driving. The risk is greatest when the phone is hand-held but still significant when it is hands-free, because the driver visualises the disembodied other party and cannot see the road or its obstacles.

Let us, therefore, get the priorities in the right order. We should stop the parents using mobiles in the car, not the children using them in the street.

The serious threats to the health of children — apart from being run over by an adult driving without due care and attention — include teenage pregnancy, drugs and abduction. The trick is how to balance information and education with allowing children to take responsibility for their own choices.

One of the joys of mobile phones — all right, well not joy exactly — is that they do allow the parents of teenagers to give them some independence while preserving an invisible electronic umbilical cord.

(Editorial, *The Independent*, 12 May 2000)

Answers to Exercise 13 are given on pp. 169–77.

Chapter 3

Recognising implications

Drawing conclusions

One important aspect of reasoning is the ability to go further than the information you have been given, to draw conclusions from evidence, to see what follows from statements which other people make. This is an ability which we all exercise to a certain extent in our daily lives. If we draw back the curtains in the morning, and find that last night's snow covering has gone, we conclude that the temperature must have risen overnight. If we know that a friend has completed a 150 mile car journey in two hours, we conclude that they must have exceeded the 70 mph speed limit.

Sometimes our conclusions will be more tentative than in these two examples. If we know that a colleague's children have all had bad colds recently, and we hear that colleague sneezing throughout the day, then it is reasonable to conclude that they have caught a cold. But they may not be suffering from a cold. Perhaps their sneezing is caused by an allergy to something in the office, for example, a new pot plant or a new type of printing ink. In cases like this, where the evidence points to a conclusion which may need to be reconsidered in the light of further evidence, it is best to express our conclusion as something which is 'probable' or 'likely'.

To improve our capacity for critical reasoning, we need to exercise the ability to draw conclusions in a systematic way whenever we are presented with information – in discussions with others, when reading newspapers and textbooks, when listening to the comments of politicians. We may find it easiest to draw conclusions about those subjects with which we are most familiar, but with practice, we can make progress in improving the ability in relation to less familiar topics.

Let us turn to some examples to illustrate this. Consider the following passage:

> Men with low blood cholesterol levels are more likely to develop intestinal cancer than those with high blood cholesterol levels. But men who have high blood cholesterol levels have an above-average risk of suffering a heart attack.
>
> (Law School Admission Test, December 1984)

What conclusions can be drawn from this information? Can we conclude that it would be a good thing for all men to aim to have a low blood cholesterol level, on the grounds that this would reduce their risk of suffering a heart attack? No, not from the information available, because if they achieved a low blood cholesterol level they would be more likely to develop intestinal cancer. So the most which can be concluded is that lowering a patient's blood cholesterol level in order to reduce the risk of heart attack may increase the patient's risk of intestinal cancer, and thus that it may not be wise to attempt to lower a patient's blood cholesterol level.

Note the tentative nature of this conclusion. It is possible that further information might lead us to revise the conclusion. Suppose that intestinal cancer is a disease which usually occurs in old age. In that case, lowering someone's blood cholesterol level may move them out of the group likely to die relatively young from a heart attack, and into the group likely to live much longer, but also at risk of – eventually – developing intestinal cancer. In that case, it may be wise to attempt to lower the blood cholesterol levels of those likely to suffer heart attacks.

Let us look at another example:

> Repeated spraying with the insecticide did not rid the tobacco fields of the insect. Only the strongest of the species survived each spraying. When they mated, they produced offspring more resistant to the insecticide than they were.
>
> (Law School Admission Test, June 1983)

What can be concluded from this information? We know that the insects which were strong enough to survive repeated spraying with insecticide produced offspring with even greater resistance to the insecticide. In the original population of insects, there were obviously some with weak resistance and some with strong resistance, so perhaps it is just a matter of chance whether a particular insect has strong or weak resistance, and therefore just a matter of chance that the offspring of the survivors had strong resistance.

But if it were just a matter of chance, then we should expect the new generation to include some insects with weak resistance to the insecticide. The fact that they all had strong resistance suggests that there is something about being the offspring of those with strong resistance which makes insects more likely to have strong resistance. And this suggests that resistance to insecticide, in at least some species, can be passed from one generation of insects to the next. This is a useful conclusion to draw because it tells us that repeated spraying with insecticide may not have the effect of eventually eliminating insect pests. It may even have the effect of making the insect population stronger, if those which have the resistance to the insecticide are strong in other respects as well, for example, in their abilities to reproduce or to withstand adverse weather conditions and disease.

Here are some exercises for you to practise your skill in drawing conclusions:

Exercise 14: Drawing conclusions

For each of the following, say what conclusion you can draw from the passage:

1   The pond is frozen this morning. It was not frozen yesterday.

2   There is a flu epidemic sweeping through the school. Gitta, one of the pupils, has a very high temperature and aching muscles, both of which are symptoms of flu.

3   The winter has been very severe. When we have a severe winter, the daffodils usually come into flower late.

4   Jane arrived before Jim, although they set off at the same time, and they were both travelling by car.

5   The murder victim died at 9 p.m. on Saturday. It is suspected that he may have been poisoned, but it is not yet known whether it was poison or the blow to his head which killed him. The injury to the head would have caused death instantly, had he still been alive when he was hit. It has now been discovered that Ms Brown, the chief suspect, was with friends 5 miles away from the murder scene between 7 p.m. and 10 p.m. on Saturday.

Answers to Exercise 14 are given on p. 177.

Exercise 15: Assessing implications

For each of the following passages, assume that what is said in the passage is true, and assess whether each of the responses (a) to (e) is *true*, *false*, *probably true*, *probably false*, or whether you have *insufficient information* in the passage to draw any conclusion about the statement's truth or falsity. Write your answer – *T, F, PT, PF*, or *II* – at the end of each of the sentences (a) to (e). You may find it interesting to compare your answers to the exercise with someone else's.

1   A study from Sweden reports that the incidence of skin cancer increased by 50 per cent between 1979 and 1987. Exposure to sunlight is known to cause skin cancer in light-skinned people. The incidence of skin cancer was found to be higher amongst professionals than amongst manual workers – thus it was higher amongst those who can afford to take holidays in places with very sunny climates. Twenty per cent of skin cancer cases occurred amongst those aged between 20 and 39, although most types of cancer are uncommon in this age group.

(from 'Cancer threats all around us', Celia Hall,
The Independent, 30 March, 1993)

(a)   Manual workers in Sweden have no risk of getting skin cancer.

(b)   There is a lower risk of skin cancer for those aged over forty than for those aged under forty.

(c)   The increase in the incidence of skin cancer in Sweden indicates that exposure to sunlight cannot be the only cause of skin cancer.

(d)   Those aged over 40 in Sweden are more likely than the rest of the population to take holidays in places with sunny climates.

(e)   The increased incidence of skin cancer in Sweden may be due to an increase in the numbers of people taking holidays in places with sunny climates.

2   Nearly 600 people, most of whom had an inflated sense of their own safety as car drivers, took part in a study which investigated ways of getting people to drive more safely. The drivers were asked to fill in a questionnaire detailing an imaginary accident which they had caused and which had serious repercussions, such as the loss of a child's life. They had to write a description of the consequences,

and imagine the subsequent guilt, lack of confidence or inability to drive again. Before the study, 50 per cent of the group said they would be prepared to drive at over 80 miles per hour on a motorway. After completion of the questionnaire, this figure fell to 27 per cent. The group most likely to overestimate their driving skills and safety were young men.

(from 'Imagining accident curbs bad drivers', Steve Connor, *The Independent*, 5 November 1993)

(a)   Most drivers have an inflated sense of their own safety.

(b)   Some drivers who overestimate their driving skills tend to drive too fast.

(c)   People with only a few years driving experience do not overestimate their skills.

(d)   Forcing drivers to imagine that they have had a serious road accident may make them drive more responsibly in the future.

(e)   Imagining that one has caused a serious accident has the undesirable effect of reducing one's confidence as a driver.

3   A technique for inducing phantom sheep pregnancies has been developed to address the problem of what to do with the million lambs born each year to mothers which for one reason or another cannot breast-feed them. Fostering is notoriously difficult because a ewe quickly forms a bond with its own lamb and rejects all others. Farmers are forced to rear orphaned lambs themselves, and lack of maternal contact can cause behaviour abnormalities. Gently stretching the neck of the cervix with two fingers sends nerve signals to the animal's brain that mimic those produced in labour. The sheep believes it has given birth to a second lamb. The orphaned lamb can then be introduced to its new mother with an 80 per cent chance that it will be accepted.

('Ewes "fooled" into acting as mothers', Steve Connor, *The Independent*, 22 March 1993)

(a)   A ewe which gives birth to two lambs from one pregnancy will form bonds with both lambs.

(b)   A ewe will reject her own lamb if she is introduced to an orphaned lamb.

(c)   An orphaned lamb may fail to develop normal behaviour if it is not fostered by a ewe.

(d) An orphaned lamb needs maternal contact in order to grow to adulthood.

(e) The formation of a bond between a ewe and a lamb can occur even if the ewe is not the mother of the lamb.

4 Dipping of sheep protects the animals from scab and blowfly attacks. Leather manufacturers report that since sheep dipping ceased to be compulsory last year, 60 per cent of British sheepskins have been found to have damage from these parasites. But there are worries that sheep dips can cause health problems for farmers who use them. The Veterinary Products Committee examined medical evidence on 266 cases of people who believed that their influenza-like symptoms were caused by exposure to sheep dip. They found a possible link to sheep dip in only fifty-eight of these cases, and of these fifty-eight, only three had worn protective clothing while using the dip. The long-term effects of low level exposure to sheep dip are not known. However, because of concerns about safety, the Ministry of Agriculture has introduced legislation requiring farmers who use sheep dips to have a certificate of competence.

('Sheep dip use to be limited to qualified farmers',
Oliver Gillie, *The Independent*, 2 December 1993)

(a) Scab and blowfly cause distress to sheep.

(b) There is no evidence that there may be a link between influenza-like symptoms and the use of sheep dips.

(c) Protective clothing prevents sheep dip from damaging farmers' health.

(d) Low level exposure to sheep dip is known to be dangerous enough to justify banning the use of the dip.

(e) Sheep dips need to be handled with great care because they present a risk to the health of farmers who use them.

Answers to Exercise 15 are given on pp. 177–80.

Recognising implications of arguments

Sometimes a whole argument has implications which go beyond the particular subject with which it is concerned. There are two important ways in which an argument can do this – by exhibiting a particular structure or shape, which it can have in common with arguments on other topics, or by relying on a general principle which can be applied to other cases. The skills involved in dealing with implications of arguments can be described as *recognising parallel arguments* and *recognising and applying principles*.

Recognising parallel arguments

The value of this skill is that being able to recognise parallel arguments may help us to see what is wrong with an argument. Sometimes it is easier for us to recognise a flaw in an argument if the argument is about a familiar subject. Suppose you are presented with an argument on an unfamiliar topic, and although you doubt your ability to assess the subject matter, you can nevertheless see that the argument has a particular shape or pattern. If you can substitute some familiar subject matter into this pattern, you may be able to see whether the argument is good. Not all arguments can be dealt with in this way; those which can tend to be relatively short, and to succeed or fail in virtue of their structure, rather than because there is additional evidence which counts against them.

Someone who objects to an argument by saying 'You might as well argue that . . .' is often presenting a parallel argument to show that there is a problem with the original argument. This is what is happening in the two following examples of conversations:

1   *James*: I mean what I say because I say what I mean.
    John: You might as well argue that you eat what you see because you see what you eat.

2   *Sam*: We have all had the experience of being deceived by our senses – the stick which looks bent when it is straight, and so on – and all the information we get through our senses in this way is potentially illusory, therefore sense experience is always unreliable.
    Jo: You might as well argue that since we've all had the experience of being lied to – that even lovers lie and that everyone is potentially untrustworthy, therefore no one can ever be trusted.

The argument presented in Exercise 5 (p. 24) offers an example in which, if we construct a parallel argument, we can see that an unwarranted inference has been made. The argument concerned the claim that there is no justification for public discussion and condemnation of the sex life of the US President. In order to persuade us that a husband who deceives his wife can nevertheless be a good President, it gave examples of Presidents who had been good husbands (in the sense that they did not deceive their wives) but bad Presidents. We could summarise this section of the argument as follows:

> Someone who does not deceive his wife can nevertheless be a bad President. So someone who does deceive his wife can be a good President.

Although the conclusion here may be true, and although – especially if we agree with the conclusion – we may be tempted to think that a good reason has been offered for it, in fact the first sentence is not a good reason for accepting the conclusion.

This is evident if we look at the following parallel argument:

> Someone who is not cruel to children can nevertheless be a bad child-minder. So someone who is cruel to children can be a good childminder.

We can immediately see with this example that the conclusion cannot be true, because someone who is cruel to children cannot possibly be a good childminder. If the conclusion must be false, then this cannot be a good argument even if the reason offered is true. The reason no doubt is true, because in order to be a good childminder you have to do more than merely refrain from cruelty to children. The argument is bad because the reason is not sufficient to establish the conclusion, and if this is so with the argument about childminders, then it is also the case with the parallel argument about US Presidents. Whether or not a President who deceives his wife can nevertheless be a good President depends upon whether the tendency to deceive extends to all areas of the President's life. It does not depend upon whether a President who is an exemplary husband deceives the public about some of his actions.

Exercise 16: Identifying parallel arguments

In these multiple choice questions, you should pick the answer which uses reasoning parallel to the reasoning in the original passage.

1   Because heroin addicts usually have one or more needle marks on their arms, and Robert has some needle marks on his arm, it follows that Robert is probably a heroin addict.

Which of the following most closely parallels the reasoning used in the argument above?

(a)   Because patients with malaria usually have high fevers, and George is a patient with malaria, George probably has a high fever.

(b)   Because patients with malaria usually have high fevers, malaria probably causes high fevers.

(c)   Because doctors have high incomes, and people with high incomes pay high taxes, doctors probably pay high taxes.

(d)   Because students are usually under twenty-five years old, and Harold is under twenty-five years old, Harold is probably a student.

(e)   Because heroin addicts usually have needle marks on their arms, most heroin addicts probably inject the drug directly into their veins.

(Law School Admission Test, February 1986)

2   It has usually been claimed that in eras of high infant mortality, parents adopted indifference to children as an emotional defence. But some scholars deny that parents were indifferent to children because so many died, arguing instead that the children died because their parents were so unconcerned about their children as to spare no time for them.

Which of the following is most similar in its structure to the argument described *in the last sentence above*?

(a)   It was not the school's new reading programme, but parents' increased concern with their children's schoolwork that produced better reading scores.

(b)   It is not true that the lack of qualified workers depresses wages in the poor sectors of an industrial economy; rather, the low wages attract unskilled labour.

(c)   It is not changing demand that prompts the introduction of new fashions; actually the clothing industry brings in new fashions whether the public wants them or not.

(d)   It is not true that those who take illegal drugs harm only themselves; by supporting organised crime, they harm society as well.

(e) It was not considered worthy of a poet to write for the Elizabethan theatre; nevertheless, many poets did so.

(Law School Admission Test, June 1983)

3 The achievement of zero population growth in Great Britain has not forestalled the recent political and economic decline of Great Britain. We must conclude that rapid population growth is not the economic disaster social scientists have led us to believe it to be.

Which of the following is most like the argument above?

(a) Many people who do not smoke cigarettes develop chronic respiratory illnesses; therefore, cigarette smoking cannot be the health risk it is supposed to be.

(b) Jerry bought expensive paint but she still had to apply two coats to the wall to cover the old colour; therefore, you might as well buy the cheapest paint available.

(c) Even if the country uses less energy this year than it did last year, more oil will be imported than was imported last year; therefore, energy conservation should be encouraged.

(d) This drug causes certain side effects in a small percentage of the population; we can conclude that it is safe for the majority of people.

(e) Some of his paintings are dull and uninspired; we can conclude that he is not in the same class as the greatest artists.

(Law School Admission Test, September 1984)

Answers to Exercise 16 are given on pp. 180–2.

Recognising and applying principles

Arguments which rely on general principles have implications beyond their own subject matter, because it is in the nature of a general principle that it is applicable to more than one case. A piece of reasoning may use such a principle without explicitly describing it as a general principle, so we need to be alert to the fact that some of the statements in an argument may apply to cases other than the one under discussion. There can be many kinds of principle, for example, legal rules, moral guidelines, business practices, and so on. Principles may function in an argument as reasons, as conclusions or as unstated assumptions. So, when we are going through the usual process of identifying reasons, conclusions and assumptions, we should ask ourselves whether any of them is a statement with general applicability.

The skill of identifying principles is valuable, because sometimes the application of a principle to other cases – that is to say, the further implications of a principle – may show us that the principle needs to be modified, or maybe even rejected. Suppose, for example, someone wants to argue against the use of capital punishment, and offers as a reason 'Killing is wrong'. This principle, stated as it is without any qualification, obviously has very wide applicability. It applies to all cases of killing. So, if we are to accept it as a principle to guide our actions, it means that killing in wartime is wrong, and killing in self-defence is wrong. If we are convinced that killing in self-defence cannot be wrong, then we have to modify our original principle in order to take account of exceptions to it. Applying principles involves being consistent in our reasoning, recognising all the implications of our own and others' reasoning.

Another example is offered by a debate in the sphere of medical ethics. It has been suggested that when the demand for treatment for illness exceeds the resources available, and thus decisions have to be made about priorities, one type of illness which should come very low on the list of priorities for treatment is illness which individuals brings upon themselves by their actions or lifestyles. Such illness can be described as 'self-inflicted'. Most doctors would *not* take the view that self-inflicted illness should not be treated, but it is an issue which is often mentioned when public opinion is consulted about how best to use the resources available for health care. For example, someone may say, 'We should not give high priority to expensive heart treatments for smokers, because they have brought their illness on themselves'.

Clearly the principle underlying this is that 'We should not give high priority to the treatment of self-inflicted illness', and it is a principle with wider applicability. But in order to understand to which cases of illness it properly applies, we need to be clearer about what exactly is meant by 'self-inflicted illness'. At the very least it must mean an illness which has been caused by the actions or behaviour of the person who is ill. On this definition, the principle would apply to a very wide range of illnesses – for example, smoking related diseases, alcohol and drug related diseases, diseases caused by unsuitable diet, some sports injuries, some road accident injuries, some cases of sexually transmitted disease. However, it may be claimed that one cannot properly be said to have *inflicted* a disease on oneself unless one *knew* that the action or behaviour would cause the illness, or it may be claimed that a disease cannot properly be said to be *self*-inflicted, if the action which caused the disease was carried out under some kind of compulsion or addiction.

So, perhaps one would wish to modify the definition of 'self-inflicted illness' to read, 'an illness which has knowingly been caused by the deliberate and free action of an individual'. This definition would give the principle narrower applicability. For example, it would not be applicable to diseases caused by bad diet when the individual did not know the effects of a bad diet. Nor would it apply to cases of illness caused by addiction. But we may still find that those cases to which it did apply – for example, a motorcyclist injured in a road accident through not wearing a crash helmet – suggested to us that there was something wrong with the principle.

Exercise 17: Applying and evaluating principles

For each of the following principles, think of a case to which it applies, and consider whether this particular application suggests to you that the principle should be modified or abandoned. This exercise would work well as the basis for a class discussion.

1   No one should have to subsidise, through taxation, services which they themselves never use.

2   We should not have laws to prevent people from harming themselves, provided their actions do not harm others.

3   There should be absolute freedom for the newspapers to publish anything they wish.

4   Doctors should be completely honest with their patients.

5   You should never pass on information which you have promised to keep secret.

Answers to Exercise 17 are given on pp. 182–3.

Chapter 4

Two skills in the use of language

Our earlier discussions of examples have relied upon the exercise of a skill which has not yet been explicitly mentioned – the understanding of language. This, of course, lies behind anyone's ability in critical thinking, since to think critically essentially involves dealing with reasoning which is expressed in language. Different individuals have differing levels of skill in dealing with language, but this is another skill which can improve with practice. You can extend your vocabulary, and increase your ability to deal with complex sentence structure. No specific exercises are offered in this book to practise these abilities, but this chapter will deal with two skills in language use which are directly related to reasoning well – the ability to use language with clarity and precision, and the ability to summarise someone else's reasoning.

The first of these skills is one which a good reasoner will have to possess, because sometimes the evaluation of reasoning crucially depends upon the clarification of the exact meaning of a word or phrase. The second skill – being able to summarise reasoning – is concerned primarily with understanding, rather than evaluating, reasoning. But since evaluation is not possible without understanding, and since summarising is a useful aid to understanding, the development of this skill will be of great value.

Using language with clarity and precision

It is in the nature of the English language that words can have more than one meaning, and thus that sometimes the use of a word, or of a phrase, can be ambiguous. One trick upon which people sometimes rely when presenting an argument is to use an ambiguous word deliberately in order to lead people to accept a conclusion which the reasoning offered does not entitle them to draw. What is supposed to be a classic example of this trick appears in the following extract from *Utilitarianism* by John Stuart Mill.

> The only proof capable of being given that an object is visible is that people actually see it. The only proof that a sound is audible is that people hear it: and so of the other sources of experience. In like manner, I apprehend, the sole evidence it is possible to produce that anything is desirable, is that people do actually desire it.
>
> (J. S. Mill, *Utilitarianism*, Collins/Fontana, p. 288)

The ambiguous word here is 'desirable', and critics of Mill claim that in this passage, given the comparison of 'desirable' with 'visible' and 'audible', the meaning of 'desirable' must be 'can be desired'. Yet, they say, Mill goes on to use this passage as a basis for the claim that happiness is 'desirable' in the sense that it 'ought to be desired'. In order to assess whether Mill really is attempting to play this trick, you would need to read Chapter 4 of *Utilitarianism*, where you may find more clues in the text as to the exact meaning which Mill intended. But for our purposes the example serves to illustrate the way in which a word may be used ambiguously.

Not all cases of ambiguity are deliberate. We looked at the following argument in Chapter 2:

> If cigarette advertising is banned, cigarette manufacturers will save the money they would otherwise have spent on advertising. Thus, in order to compete with each other, they will reduce the price of cigarettes. So, banning cigarette advertising will be likely to lead to an increase in smoking.

We noted that it was not clear whether the phrase 'an increase in smoking' meant that the numbers of people who smoke would increase, or that those who smoke would smoke more, or both. There is no particular reason to think that this phrase has been left unclear deliberately in order to persuade us to accept an otherwise ill-founded conclusion. The person presenting the argument may have had a very clear idea as to what they meant by the phrase, and may have believed that the argument gave strong support to the conclusion. Perhaps the exact meaning of the phrase was not spelt out because the author did not notice the ambiguity. In this short passage, there are no further clues as to what the author might have meant.

In such cases we need to evaluate both possible interpretations. Would a reduction in the price of cigarettes be likely to persuade more people to smoke? This is questionable, since it seems unlikely that what deters people from smoking is the price of cigarettes. Amongst those who do not smoke, there are, presumably, some who have never wanted to do so, and some who have given up smoking solely because of the health risks. For people in these two categories, the cost of cigarettes plays no part in their motivations. It is just possible – but very unlikely – that some ex-smokers would return to smoking, if only cigarettes were cheaper. It is possible, and a little more likely, that some non-smokers – perhaps young people who have not yet developed the habit – would become smokers if cigarettes were cheaper.

Let us turn to the other interpretation – would a reduction in the price of cigarettes be likely to result in smokers smoking more? This is possible. There may be some smokers who restrict the number of cigarettes they smoke per day because they are expensive, who would like to smoke more, and who think that a few more cigarettes per day would not increase the health risks which they already incur.

We have seen two examples where an ambiguous word or phrase is used. In such cases, we need to look for clues in the text as to which interpretation is intended. If we are unable to find such clues, we need to evaluate the reasoning in relation to each of the possible interpretations.

Another type of case in which clarification is required is where a term is used which is clearly intended to encompass a whole class of objects, but since the term has not been precisely defined in the text, it is not clear exactly what things it covers. An example was presented in the last chapter, under the discussion of the application of principles. The principle in question was 'We should not give high priority to the treatment of self-inflicted illness'. It would not be possible to evaluate reasoning which relied on this principle until we had clarified the exact definition of the term 'self-inflicted illness'. Sometimes in such cases there will be clues in the text as to what the author's definition must be. Where we can find no such clues, we must consider all the definitions which we think are possible, and assess the reasoning based upon each of these in turn.

Exercise 18: Clarifying words or phrases

For each of the following passages, identify any word or phrase which is crucial to the reasoning, and which you think needs to be clarified. Identify the different possible interpretations of the word or phrase, and assess the difference they make to the reasoning in the passage:

1   What makes a beautiful face? How long or short should the perfect
     nose be; is there an optimal length to the face or ear lobe; what
     should the angle of the eyes be in respect to the bridge of the nose?
     Recent research suggests that beauty is simply a matter of being
     Mr or Ms average.
          Three hundred psychology students were asked to rate pictures
     of faces using an attractiveness score of one to five. Some of the
     pictures were of a single individual, and some were composite faces,
     made up from the features of 2, 4, 8, 16 or up to 32 individual
     faces. The lowest scores for attractiveness were those for individual
     faces. The attractiveness ratings increased with increases in the
     number of faces which were used to make a composite face.
          So, take heart! Beauty is only the sum total of our big and
     little noses, receding and protruding chins, high and low foreheads.
     In order to be beautiful you do not have to be unusual − you only
     have to be average after all.

2   It is important that in bringing up children we should try to develop
     in them the quality of empathy, because those who lack it can be
     dangerous. For example, child molesters and psychopaths are dan-
     gerous precisely because they do not care about the suffering of
     others. However, children will need more than the quality of empathy
     in order to grow up into the kind of citizens we want, because
     empathy can be used in good or evil ways − for example by the
     businessman who can use his understanding of others in order to
     inspire colleagues or in order to exploit them.

3   Doctors should always be honest with their patients. If a doctor tells
     a patient a lie, and she finds out that she has been deceived, then
     the relationship of trust which is crucial for successful medical treat-
     ment will have broken down. Moreover since patients have a right
     to be know everything about their medical condition, those patients
     who ask doctors about their condition should be given truthful
     answers to their questions.

Answers to Exercise 18 are given on pp. 183–4.

Summarising arguments

For most of the examples in this book, we have set out the structure of arguments simply by using the exact wording of the passages under consideration. In doing so, we have picked out the relevant parts of a passage – basic reasons and intermediate conclusions (both stated and unstated), and main conclusions – and set them out in a way which shows the progression of the reasoning. This may be quite easy to do with short passages, especially if they have very clear conclusion indicators and reason indicators. But with longer pieces, such as are often found in newspapers, you need a clear understanding of the whole passage before you can attempt to set out all the steps in the reasoning. Writing a summary can help with this understanding in two ways. First, having to express something in your own words forces you to come to grips with exactly what the passage is saying. Second, the particular kind of summary we recommend helps you to make a long argument more manageable by breaking it down into smaller stages.

First pick out the main conclusion, either by identifying conclusion indicators, or by asking 'What is the main message which this passage is trying to get me to believe or accept?' Then pick out the *immediate* reasons which are intended to support this. These could be basic reasons and/or intermediate conclusions. Don't try to summarise all the reasoning at this stage – for example, do not try to work out exactly how the intermediate conclusions (if any) are supported. Just concentrate on the one or two (or three, or more) statements immediately supporting the main conclusion. Then express the main conclusion and the statements supporting it in your own words.

Your summary could have the following form:

The passage is trying to get me to accept that .... (main conclusion) ...., on the grounds that .... (intermediate conclusion 1) .... and .... (basic reason) .... and .... (intermediate conclusion 2).

When you have written this first brief summary, you will have a framework into which you can fit the more detailed reasoning. You can then take each intermediate conclusion in turn, and ask what reasons are offered in support of it.

Let's apply this to an example:

Example 1: Nicotine for smokers

Nicotine products, such as nicotine gum and nicotine patches, should be made available cheaply, widely advertised and given endorsement from health authorities. This would make it likely that smokers would transfer their addiction to these less harmful products.

It is the impurities in tobacco which cause cancer, accounting for one-third of cancer deaths in Britain per year, whereas the nicotine in tobacco provides pleasure, stimulation and stress relief. Although the impurities in tobacco could be removed, it is unlikely that the tobacco industry will clean up its product as long as sales of tobacco are buoyant.

It is thought that nicotine may be a contributory cause of heart disease. But the benefits to health from giving up tobacco are likely to outweigh the risks of taking nicotine.

What is the main message which this passage is trying to get us to accept? It is clearly concerned with the idea that nicotine products should be promoted, as a means of trying to get smokers to stop smoking tobacco.

The immediate reason it gives for promoting nicotine is that doing so would make it more likely that smokers would switch from harmful tobacco to less harmful nicotine products. So our first attempt at a summary would be:

The passage is trying to get me to accept that nicotine products should be made available cheaply, widely advertised, and given endorsement from health authorities, on the grounds that these products are less harmful than tobacco, and that promoting them would make it likely that smokers would stop smoking and use these products instead.

We have extracted two reasons here from the second sentence – that the products are less harmful than tobacco, and that promoting them would change smokers' behaviour. The rest of the passage is principally concerned with giving support to the first of these reasons – trying to show that these products *are* less harmful than tobacco. But paragraphs two and three can also be seen as lending some support to an unstated intermediate conclusion that if smokers knew more about which components of tobacco give them pleasure, and which put them at risk of cancer, they would switch to using nicotine products other than tobacco, especially if nicotine patches and gum were relatively cheap.

Example 2: Subsidising the arts

Now let's try summarising a longer passage:

Some people maintain that there is no case for subsidising the arts because they are a minority interest. In its most sympathetic guise, this view presents itself as defending the poor. What subsidy for the arts amounts to is taking money from all the taxpayers (including those who never set foot in a museum or theatre, let alone the Royal Opera House) to help pay for the leisure activities of the privileged classes. And why, they say, should we subsidise snobbish entertainments such as opera when we don't subsidise proletarian ones such as football?

Quite apart from the patronising assumption that most ordinary people are permanently immune to culture, however inexpensive it might be made by subsidy (free in the case of most museums), there is an odd anomaly in this argument. Taken to its logical conclusion, it would undermine any kind of taxation in a democratic society. What is the difference between claiming that people should not have to pay for the arts if they never use them and saying that they should not have to support the school system if they are childless, or pay for road building if they have no car?

The way we collect and spend taxes is not based on the same principle as paying for private services. If the country decides that it believes certain things, whether universal schooling or the preservation of its cultural heritage, to be for the good of the nation as a whole, it does not require that every single taxpayer partake of those good things.

So why is art a good thing? Why is it so important that Covent Garden be given millions of pounds of our money, even though so few of us go to the opera, when thousands of people who prefer to play golf have to pay for it themselves? Why should my pastime be more worthy than yours?

John Stuart Mill was compelled to modify the simplistic utilitarian principle that good consisted in 'the greatest happiness of the greatest number', because it implied that all pleasures were equal: that pushpin was as good as poetry. The arts are not just an eccentric kind of hobby.

As I have written before when defending art against philistines from within, what the arts offer us is a way both of making sense of our condition and of transcending it. They are, in the end, what makes us human rather than bestial.

(Taken from an article which appeared in *The Times* on 12 October 1995 (© Janet Daley) reproduced by permission of A. M. Heath & Co. Ltd.)

What is this passage trying to get us to accept? It discusses one type of argument against subsidising the arts from public money, and says that 'there is an odd anomaly in this argument'. It also seeks to explain why art is a good thing – the kind of thing which can be judged to be for the good of the nation as a whole. So clearly it is trying to convince us that one argument against subsidising the arts is a bad argument, and that there is a positive reason for subsidising the arts. Our first summary could be as follows:

> The passage is trying to get me to accept that subsiding the arts is a good thing, on the grounds that, like universal schooling, the arts are good for the nation as a whole, and things which are good for the nation as a whole should be subsidised from public money, even though some people who pay taxes may never use these services.

Two immediate reasons have been identified here – that the arts are good for the nation, and that it is appropriate to subsidise things which are good for the nation even if some taxpayers do not use them.

The first of these reasons is given support by the claim that the arts 'are, in the end, what makes us human rather than bestial'. The second reason is supported by showing the implications of the principle sometimes used to defend the claim that we should not subsidise the arts – that principle being that we should not subsidise from taxes those services which some taxpayers do not use. This would mean that taxes should not be used to subsidise education and road building because some taxpayers don't have children, and some don't drive cars. Since (it is assumed) these implications are unacceptable, the principle from which they follow should be rejected, and we should accept instead the principle that things which are good for the nation as a whole should be subsidised from tax revenue.

In these two examples, we have offered an initial simple summary, which does not seek to set out all the steps of the argument, but aims to identify the principal reasons which give immediate support to the main conclusion. We have then shown how, with this first brief summary as a basis, we can fill in the reasoning in a more detailed way. The following exercise gives you a chance to practise doing this.

In some particularly long or complex passages (for example, some of those in Exercise 20) you may find it helpful to look first for themes in different sections of the passage, and to summarise each theme before you try to summarise the main conclusion and reasons.

Exercise 19: Writing a summary

For each of the following passages:

(a) write a summary of the main conclusion and the immediate reasons (basic reasons or intermediate conclusions) offered for it;

(b) identify the reasoning which is meant to support any intermediate conclusion you have identified.

1   There is something revolting about the idea of killing for pleasure. No matter how much the hunting lobby bray about the thrill of the chase and the skill of the riders, one simple fact remains: the end purpose of this sport is death. Killing for food, killing for protection, killing to manage the countryside; all these are essential and we shouldn't be squeamish about them. But the idea that people could be so proud of enjoying the kill is rather repellent.

Tradition is no defence. The fact that families have been playing such games for centuries doesn't justify their heirs continuing to hunt today. For centuries people have been doing all sorts of appalling things – including badger baiting, cockfighting and working ponies until they dropped – that we have now made illegal. Compassion about animals isn't a fad for flaky urbanites, nor is it simply squeamishness; it is a measure of a society becoming gentler and more civilised. This newspaper wouldn't hunt.

But would we therefore ban it? We would not; the prospect of the state intervening to ban an activity where the harm to others is not overwhelming, troubles us deeply.

For a start, the cruelty case against fox-hunting is not clear cut. Foxes are not as fluffy as they look. Basil Brush and Roald Dahl – author of the children's classic, *Fantastic Mr Fox* – may have helped the little vermin weave their way into our affections, but they are predators which have been controlled for centuries by farmers and landowners, rich and poor. The anti-hunting lobby needs to make a more convincing case that other methods of slaughtering foxes are genuinely less cruel than hunting, before the arguments for a ban become overwhelming.

('Beware of the anti-hunting roundheads in full cry' –
comment, *The Independent*, 24 December 1996)

2   The business lobby risks crying wolf once too often over the Government's plans to give fathers a fortnight's paid paternity leave . . .

New dads in Britain actually increase their hours of work. They are hardly shirkers – they work the longest hours in Europe. Would it do so much harm to let them get to know their babies for a couple of weeks before returning to the treadmill?

If that sounds too sentimental, then think practically. The NHS pushes mothers out of maternity wards as soon as possible. Who looks after them? Up to 20 per cent of these women have had Caesarean deliveries. Many lack extended families to back them up. Fathers are a key support. It is hardly surprising that post-natal depression is less prevalent when the father is actively involved.

Breast-feeding is apparently more successful when dads are more supportive and well-informed. This is why the health service in Scotland targets dads in its public health education programme. It also points to a vital purpose for paternity leave. During the first fortnight, ham-fisted first-time parents gain both confidence and some knowledge. Health visitors are in and out of the home. But if dad is at work, he misses out, and so may his children.

Does it matter that so many fathers are ignorant of the basics in child care? It does, when you stop to realise that more and more children are in the sole care of their fathers more of the time. The latest research shows that where mothers are working, fathers now do more care-giving than any other third party. In short, ignorant fathers are a danger to their children.

If this is still too sentimental for the business lobby, then let's talk profit. AMP, Australia's largest insurer, gives its new dads six weeks' paid parental leave, far more than the Government's parsimonious proposal. They reckon the scheme saves them money through reduced staff turnover. Looking after dads is not just good for families, it can be good for business.

('Paternity leave is good for families and good for business' – comment, *The Independent*, 8 December 2000)

3   Organs for transplantation are in very short supply, and in most countries demand greatly exceeds supply. In Austria and Spain, however, the situation is very much better as there is 'presumed consent' in relation to organs that can be taken from someone who has died; that is, unless an individual has made an official deposition to the contrary, any organ can be taken for transplantation when they are dead.

This seems to me to be an altruism-encouraging piece of legislation that other countries ought to copy.

It is also regarded as noble and altruistic to donate an organ to a friend or relative. Such transplants negate the idea that our bodies are somehow sacred and nothing should be taken from them.

So, given the acceptance of organ donation and the emphasis on patient autonomy, why is there horror and almost universal rejection of the possibility of a person selling their kidney for money? If patients have the rights over their own bodies, why should they not be allowed to do what they like with them? It does not harm anyone else. No one denies the right of people to take risks with their bodies as climbers, skiers and even urban cyclists, regularly do. Boxers are paid for us to see them suffer severe bodily damage. Soldiers protect us by risking their bodies.

The most common argument I hear is that rich people will be able to buy kidneys from poor people – to which my reply is that poor people will thus be able to get some money. I cannot see on what grounds one should not be able to sell parts of one's body apart from an almost instinctive distaste, but that is not in itself a good basis for making judgements. Imagine a situation where a desperately poor person – perhaps even in another country – could escape from debilitating poverty by sale of an organ. Such a sale, if the money were good, could transform the life of the seller's family. This could be open to abuse but could be subject to regulation in a manner analogous to the control there is over the way we sell our labour.

(Lewis Wolpert, 'Kidney trouble', *The Independent on Sunday*, 22 February 1998)

Answers to Exercise 19 are given on p. 184.

Chapter 5

Exercising the skills
of reasoning

Most of the reasoning which you will encounter and want to assess – in, for example, newspapers, journals and textbooks – will not be presented in neat, short passages typical of the majority of those in this book. Instead, you will often find that you have to extract the reasoning from a long passage which may contain some irrelevant material, and which may present reasons and conclusions in a jumbled way, rather than setting them out in what would seem to be a clear series of steps. The task of assessing a long passage also differs from most of the exercises in this book, in that, rather than focusing on one particular skill, it requires you to bring all your reasoning skills into play. You will have to play the whole game, choosing the appropriate skills, just as tennis players have to play a game, choosing whether their well practised forehand drive or their beautifully honed backhand volley is the appropriate shot.

You have already had the opportunity to practise your skills on some longer passages in Exercise 13 (p. 73). In this chapter, we shall show some examples of analysis and evaluation of long passages of reasoning, and end with some passages with which you can get to grips yourselves.

Longer passages of reasoning

Dealing with longer passages of reasoning can seem daunting at first, but it helps if we remember that the same skills are called for, whatever the length of the passage. We shall present the important steps, expanding on the list set out in Chapter 3.

1   The first task is to identify the conclusion and the reasons. You may find conclusion indicators (such as 'therefore' or 'so') and reason indicators (such as 'because' or 'since') to help you to do this. But some passages will contain no such words, and you will need to identify the conclusion by understanding the main message of the passage. So start by reading the whole passage, and asking yourself 'What is this passage trying to persuade me to accept or believe?'. When you have answered this, ask 'What immediate reasons or evidence is it presenting in order to get me to believe this?'. It may be helpful at this stage to write a brief summary, on the following lines:

> This passage is trying to get me to accept
> that ....,
> on the grounds that,
> first ....,
> second ...., and so on.

With very long passages, it may also be helpful to break the passage down into smaller sections, and look for themes in different parts of the text, before writing your summary.

2   When you have sorted out what reasons are being offered, you need to consider what assumptions are being made. These could be:

- assumptions which function as support for basic reasons, or as unstated additional reasons, or as unstated intermediate conclusions,

- assumptions about the meanings of words or phrases, so look for ambiguous words and terms which require more precise definition,

- assumptions that one case or one situation is analogous to or comparable with another, so look to see if any comparisons are being made; and

- assumptions that a particular explanation of a piece of evidence is the only plausible explanation, so look out for explanations.

In identifying assumptions, you are reconstructing the background of a particular piece of reasoning.

3   Once you are clear about the reasoning and its background, you need to evaluate it. Consider how far you can go in assessing the truth of the reasons and the unstated assumptions. Think about how you would seek further information to enable you to assess the truth of reasons.

4   Does the reasoning rely on evidence from sources whose authority is questionable?

5   Do you yourself have any knowledge which strengthens or weakens the conclusion? Or can you think of anything which *may* be true and which would have a bearing on the conclusion? (Remember to subject your own 'knowledge' to the same standards of scrutiny as you apply to the claims made by other people!)

6   If you have identified any explanations in the passage, are they plausible, and are they the only plausible explanations of what is being explained?

7   If you have found comparisons in the text, are these comparisons appropriate – that is to say, are the two things which are being compared alike in the relevant respects?

8   From the information in the passage, can you draw any important conclusions not mentioned in the passage? Do any of these conclusions suggest that the reasoning in the passage is faulty?

9   Is the reasoning in the passage (or any part of the reasoning) similar to – or parallel with – reasoning which you know to be faulty?

10   Do any of the reasons or assumptions embody a general principle? If there is any such general principle, can you think of any applications of it which would suggest that there is something wrong with the principle?

11   Assess the degree of support which the reasons and assumptions provide for the conclusion. If you believe that the conclusion is not well supported, can you state the way in which the move from reasons to conclusion is flawed? Your answers to questions 5 to 10 above may help you to do this.

This list is primarily applicable to passages which do contain a recognisable argument, with a main conclusion and with some reasons or evidence offered in support of it. It is, however, possible to find passages which contain reasoning, but do not come to a major conclusion. Perhaps they examine evidence from two opposing sides of an issue, and leave the readers to draw their own conclusions. Or perhaps they are seeking to explain something, as did the passages in Exercise 12. Even for passages without a main conclusion you will find it useful to go through the steps listed above in attempting to evaluate the reasoning.

Two examples of evaluation of reasoning

Example 1: Science versus theology

In your dismally unctuous leading article (18 March) asking for a reconciliation between science and 'theology', you remark that 'people want to know as much as possible about their origins'. I certainly hope they do, but what on earth makes you think that 'theology' has anything useful to say on the subject? Science is responsible for the following knowledge about our origins.

We know approximately when the universe began and why it is largely hydrogen. We know why stars form, and what happens in their interiors to convert hydrogen to other elements and hence give birth to chemistry in a world of physics. We know the fundamental principles of how a world of chemistry can become biology through the arising of self-replicating molecules. We know how the principle of self-replication gives rise, through Darwinian selection, to all life including humans.

It is science, and science alone, that has given us this knowledge and given it, moreover, in fascinating, overwhelming, mutually confirming detail. On every one of these questions theology has held a view that has been conclusively proved wrong. Science has eradicated smallpox, can immunise against most previous deadly viruses, can kill most previously deadly bacteria.

Theology has done nothing but talk of pestilence as the wages of sin. Science can predict when a particular comet will reappear and, to the second, when the next eclipse will occur. Science has put men on the moon and hurtled reconnaissance rockets around Saturn and Jupiter. Science can tell you the age of a particular fossil and that the Turin Shroud is a medieval fake. Science knows the precise DNA instructions of several viruses and will, in the lifetime of many present readers of *The Independent*, do the same for the human genome.

What has 'theology' ever said that is of the smallest use to anybody? When has 'theology' ever said anything that is demonstrably true and is not obvious? I have listened to theologians, read them, debated against them. I have never heard any of them ever say anything of the smallest use, anything that was not either platitudinously obvious or downright false.

If all the achievements of scientists were wiped out tomorrow there would be no doctors but witch-doctors, no transport faster than a horse, no computers, no printed books, no agriculture beyond subsistence peasant farming. If all the achievements of theologians were wiped out tomorrow, would anyone notice the smallest difference?

> Even the bad achievements of scientists, the bombs and sonar-guided whaling vessels, *work*! The achievements of theologians don't do anything, don't affect anything, don't achieve anything, don't even mean anything. What makes you think that 'theology' is a subject at all?
>
> (Letter to the Editor from Richard Dawkins,
> *The Independent,* 20 March 1993)

Let us evaluate the argument, using the eleven steps listed earlier (pp. 102–3):

1   We must first try to write a brief summary of the passage, setting out what it seeks to persuade us to accept, and the reasons it gives as to why we should accept it. We are clearly being led to believe that theology is in some way inferior to science, because whereas science can give us great deal of useful knowledge, theology cannot produce anything important or worthwhile. We could express the main theme as follows:

> This passage is trying to get me to accept that 'theology' is not a respectable subject, in the way that science is, on the grounds that science has numerous achievements, all of which work, and most of which are beneficial, whereas the achievements of theology are ineffective and meaningless.

We need to set out the reasons in a little more detail. What support is given for the idea that science is such a valuable activity? The passage mentions scientific knowledge about the origins of life and the universe, the success of science in eradicating illnesses, achievements in space exploration. It describes the restricted life we would have if the achievements of science were wiped out. It points out that even the bad achievements of science work.

How does it seek to persuade us that theology is worthless? It claims that theology has been proved wrong about the origins of human life. It suggests that theology has contributed nothing to our understanding of the causes of disease – it 'has done nothing but talk of pestilence as the wages of sin'. It claims that theology has never said anything which is not either obvious or false. It suggests that no one would notice if the achievements of theology were wiped out, and that these achievements, in contrast with even the bad achievements of science, do not work, have no effects, and have no meaning.

2   What assumptions underlie these reasons? The claim that science is responsible for 'knowledge' about our origins relies on the assumption that scientific theories – for example, theories about the origin of the universe,

and the theory of evolution – constitute knowledge. Although the bad achievements of science are mentioned, they are not regarded as evidence that science is anything but a force for good, so there is an assumption that the bad effects of science do not outweigh the good effects. The conclusion that theology is not a subject relies upon an assumption that in order for something to be a subject, it must have some effect on people's lives, or some meaning for people's lives. Some of these assumptions may immediately strike you as questionable, but we shall deal with that presently under point 3.

Are there any words or phrases whose meaning needs to be clarified? There are some scientific terms – 'self-replicating molecules', 'DNA instructions', 'human genome'. We may not know the exact meanings of these terms, and perhaps this limits our ability to assess the claim that these aspects of scientific knowledge are worthwhile. If we do not know the context of this letter, we may question exactly what is meant by theology not being a *subject*. The letter was written in response to an article which welcomed the endowment of a lectureship in theology and natural science at Cambridge University, so Dawkins' view is that theology is not respectable as a subject of academic study.

Are any comparisons made? Yes, the whole passage is about the relative merits of science and theology. In concluding that theology does not qualify as a subject, the passage must assume that science and theology are comparable in at least one respect – in that both should measure up to certain standards in order to count as subjects of academic study.

Are there explanations which rely on assumptions? The second paragraph takes for granted that the scientific explanation of the origins of human beings – based on scientific theories – is the correct explanation.

3   To what extent can we assess the truth of the reasons and unstated assumptions? Even non-scientists will have no difficulty in accepting that scientific research is responsible for advances in medical knowledge, and, if technology is to be regarded as a part of science, for many of the things (transport, computers, books, modern agriculture) which make our lives easier and more enjoyable. Non-scientists may feel ill qualified to judge whether theories about the origins of the universe and of human life have the status of knowledge, and also whether, for example, research into the DNA instructions of the human genome is valuable. We can all think of some of the bad effects of science – for example, weapons of mass destruction, pollution – and we can consider whether on balance science is a worthwhile activity.

What of the comments about the worthlessness of theology? Is it true that no one would notice if the achievements of theologians were wiped out tomorrow? Is it true that theology achieves and means nothing? Surely this is something we can find out only by investigating the role which religion plays in people's lives. Maybe the thinking and the writings of theologians are of great value to many individuals, albeit in a very different way from the way in which science is valuable.

4   To what extent does the reasoning rely on authorities? The letter does not quote any specific sources, but the comments about the achievements of science derive their authority to some extent from the fact that the letter is written by a scientist. The whole area of scientific knowledge presents us with a dilemma in relation to the assessment of the reliability of authorities. On the one hand, scientists are in a better position than non-scientists to assess the validity and, in some respects, the value of the results of scientific research. On the other hand, because their whole life's work may have been based on a particular theory, some scientists may not be in the best position to make unbiased judgements about evidence which goes against their views in a particular area of scientific knowledge. Moreover, in a discussion claiming that the whole activity of science is valuable, we would expect a scientist to emphasise those aspects favourable to the case, and perhaps play down the unfavourable aspects. Similarly we would expect a theologian to regard his or her own work as valuable. However, the case does not rest solely on Dawkins' authority as a scientist. We can all look at some of the effects of science, and consider whether the world is a better or a worse place for the existence of science.

5   What knowledge do you have which would strengthen or weaken the conclusion? We do know that science has some bad effects, and perhaps this weakens the case that we would be worse off without the achievements of science. Perhaps you know many people who find religion a great comfort in their lives, or who enjoy reading the works of theologians. This would weaken the claim that theology has no effect on anyone's lives. One could perhaps attempt to make a case for the superiority of theology over science, in that science has bad effects, whereas theology does not. However, some may point out the evil influences of some religious ideas – for example, intolerance and hostility to those who think differently. Dawkins does not take this line, in fact his claim that theology has no effects entails that it has no bad effects.

6   Is the scientific explanation of the origins of human beings more plausible than a theologian's explanation? Not all theologians will see a conflict between the two. Some Christians, for example, might say that the idea that human beings were created by God is compatible with the scientific explanation offered by the theory of evolution.

7 Does the text make any comparisons, and are they appropriate? We observed earlier that the passage assumes that in order to qualify as a 'subject', both science and theology must meet certain criteria and that theology fails to do so. One might see the text as implying that science makes an excellent job of what science is supposed to do – discovering information about the physical world, and usefully applying this information – whereas theology is hopeless at doing what science is supposed to do. But why should this disqualify it as a subject for academic study? Dawkins lists a number of scientific questions on which theologians have held mistaken views, but this is true of some scientists also, and it is possible that our view of the world will be superseded in the future.

8 We have already mentioned two conclusions we can draw from the passage, first that the bad effects of science *may* outweigh the good effects, and second that if theology has no effects, it has no bad effects.

9 Dawkins is judging theology in scientific terms, which may not be appropriate. It may be possible to construct a parallel argument about other subjects which, like theology, do not have the practical effects typical of science, but are nevertheless accepted as respectable subjects of academic study.

10 We identified the general principle that for something to be an appropriate subject of study it must have some effect on people's lives, or some meaning for people's lives. This seems a reasonable principle, provided is it broadly interpreted so that history, for example, is regarded as having meaning for people's lives.

11 The main objections to the reasoning are that the comparison between science and theology is inappropriate, in that theology should not be required to be useful *in the same sphere* as science in order for it to be a proper subject for academic study; and that theology may well satisfy the principle which requires it to have some effect on – or some meaning for – people's lives.

Example 2: Five reasons for a life of less crime

Crime. We all worry about it. President Bill Clinton used his State of the Union address this week to pledge an attack on it. Here in Britain both political parties realise that they must respond to public fears of it. The fear in America is that the very fabric of society is under siege. The fear here, where crime is lower, is that we might go down the American route.

Yet it is perfectly possible – indeed highly probable – that in Britain at least we are at one of those great turning points that occur every couple of generations: that crime, having risen inexorably since the Fifties, is now about to start a long period of decline, similar to the period from the 1830s onwards through most of the last century. Here are five reasons why this might be so.

The first is demography. Most crime is committed by young men. In 1986 there were more than 2.4 million men aged 20 to 24 in the UK, a figure which had risen from less than 2 million in 1976. This figure is now falling fast. By 1991 it was less than 2.3 million and it is projected to fall to just over 1.9 million by 1996 and slightly above 1.8 million by 2001. This is a big swing: 1.8 million will have to work roughly one-third harder to commit as many offences as 2.4 million did in the mid-Eighties.

That is a tall order. Even if these young men are even more criminally inclined than the mid-Eighties batch, and commit 10 or 15 per cent more offences per person, the crime rate will still come down.

Next, there is the trend in unemployment. Of course some of the most spectacular crimes, giant frauds for example, are committed by people in work. But there is undoubtedly some relationship between unemployment and crime, if only because people working 40 hours a week have 40 fewer hours to do anything else. The likely trend of unemployment deserves a column itself, but the demographic change ought to reduce unemployment among the young.

In any case, looked at from a long historical viewpoint the high unemployment rates of the Eighties throughout Europe are unusual. The very low rates of the Fifties are also unusual, but a return to the 5 to 8 per cent range by the end of this decade is quite possible.

Third: technology. We are only just beginning to realise the full implications of devices such as the video camera, which could be as important in cutting crime as the invention of street lighting in the last century. The pioneering work here has been done in the Scottish town of Airdrie, which introduced cameras in November 1992. A dramatic drop in crime resulted. Since then a number of cities and towns have introduced surveillance schemes or are about to. A set of cameras in Bournemouth cut vandalism to such an extent that the system paid for itself in little more than a year. The biggest such experiment is in Glasgow, and if that achieves similar results, it will show that video cameras are as effective in giant cities as in small and medium-sized ones.

Naturally there are many other technologies that will help further: technologies as varied as a national DNA register, car immobilisers and the etching of photos on credit cards. But video cameras are the big success story of the past couple of years.

Fourth: policing. It is monstrously unfair to say so, but during the Eighties the police seemed almost to boast about rising crime. They behaved like a data collection agency; the more crime they could record, the more they needed more people, higher pay and faster cars to fight it. Instead of being ashamed of their failure, they blustered on about failures of society.

It is hard to generalise, but attitudes really seem to have changed. In some specific areas, like football matches, policing has visibly improved. My colleagues on the sports desk point out that the hooting and singing by some fans during the one-minute silence for Sir Matt Busby seemed shocking because it contrasted with generally better behaviour at football matches in recent years. This they attributed not to any change in the fans but in the policing of them. Pressure on the police is probably improving performance in other areas too.

Finally: change in social attitudes, in culture, in what we all expect of people. It is hard to pin this down, but something is clearly happening. People are not only more worried; they are more angry and they are becoming more organised. In Scotland, where crime fell quite sharply last year and clear-up rates have risen, the shift is attributed by police to a number of factors, including neighbourhood watch schemes and generally better co-operation with the public.

Individually, these five points might not be sufficient to turn round what has been a steady and alarming rise in crime. There are offsetting negative forces that I have not discussed, including the greater availability of firearms which are now flooding out of the old Soviet empire; greater freedom of movement within Europe and between Britain and the rest of the world; probably still rising levels of drug abuse; the danger that better job prospects for young qualified people will leave the unqualified even more excluded and alienated.

But taken together, the five factors cutting crime ought to have greater impact than each would have individually. Once it is clear that crime really is coming down, the word gets around and a virtuous circle is established. Police and public become more confident: detection rates rise; it becomes harder to dispose of stolen goods, so the returns fall. The risk–reward ratio is thus tilted against the aspiring criminal, and crime simply becomes an unattractive proposition.

All this, please note, has nothing to do with politicians and nothing to do with the law.

The reaction of most people to this argument would probably be that, if it proves true, it should be warmly welcomed: crime is bad. It may sound odd, then, to end with a warning.

There will be costs to falling crime. The sort of changes outlined above will involve some restriction of individual liberties. It is not just that we will have to become used to being watched as we shop, or simply walk up the street. We may, a generation from now, find ourselves in a more censorious society: one which imposes greater social control on our behaviour and which becomes much more hostile to people who do not conform to what other people regard as normal and proper. Our society may become safer, but it may also become less exuberant, less interesting, and in some senses, less free.

(Hamish McRae, *The Independent*, 27 January 1994)

This article was written some time ago, and made predictions about crime figures. We need to evaluate the reasoning primarily in relation to evidence available at the time. Nevertheless it is interesting to look at its predictions with the benefit of hindsight, and in the following analysis brief comments will be made about the extent to which subsequent developments have borne out the author's claims. The example highlights the difficulties of foreseeing future developments, and yet policy decision often have to be based on such predictions.

1   The passage aims to convince us of two things, that crime is likely to decrease, and that this decrease in crime will have disadvantages as well as benefits. It presents reasoning for two separate conclusions:

> It is perfectly possible – indeed highly probable – that in Britain crime is now about to start a long period of decline.

and

> There will be costs to falling crime.

We cannot complain in this example that the reasons are difficult to find, since the passage explicitly says that there are five reasons for the first conclusion, and obligingly sets them out labelled 'The first', 'Next', 'Third', 'Fourth' and 'Finally'. These reasons are summarised below:

(a) The number of crimes committed by the age group responsible for most crime (young men) is likely to decrease.
(b) It is possible that unemployment, which has some association with crime, will decrease overall, and it ought to fall amongst the young.
(c) Effective technological aids to crime detection are being developed.
(d) Policing is becoming more effective.
(e) Social attitudes are hardening against criminals – people are becoming more organised against crime.

There is a sixth point:

> (f) Taken together, the five factors cutting crime ought to have greater impact than each would have individually.

Reason (a) is given support by figures showing that the number of men in the age group 20–24 in the UK fell from 2.4 million in 1986 to less than 2.3 million in 1991, and is predicted to fall to 1.9 million by 1996, and slightly above 1.8 million by 2001.

We are not given much to support the claim in reason (b) that unemployment will decrease overall – merely that, looked at from a historical viewpoint, the high unemployment rates of the 1980s are unusual. In order to support the claim that unemployment amongst the young will fall, the passage relies on the idea that lower numbers of people in the age group 20–24 will reduce unemployment for that group.

Reason (c) is supported by examples of the use of video cameras in Airdrie and Bournemouth, which are claimed to have resulted in a drop in crime. Other technologies which could help further are mentioned – a national DNA register, car immobilisers and the etching of photos on credit cards.

Nothing much is offered in support of reason (d), beyond the observation that the writer's colleagues who report on sport say that policing at football matches has improved.

The only support offered for reason (e) is the mention of neighbourhood watch schemes, and better co-operation between the police and the public.

Reason (f) is supported by the observation that as crime decreases, police and public become more confident, detection rates rise and crime becomes an unattractive proposition.

Now let us consider support for the second conclusion – that there will be costs to falling crime. The reasons offered are:

- The changes will involve some restriction of individual liberties – we will have to become used to being watched as we shop, or simply walk up the street.
- Society may become more censorious – more hostile to people who do not conform to what other people regard as normal and proper.

2   What assumptions underlie the reasoning? First, assumptions relating to the first conclusion. There is an assumption – an additional reason – which must be added to reason (a) – that there will probably be no increase in crimes committed by groups other than young men.

It is not immediately clear what assumption goes along with that part of reason (b) which says that 'the demographic change ought to reduce unemployment among the young', because we need to clarify what is meant here by a reduction of unemployment amongst the young. Does it mean that the percentage of under-24-year-olds who are unemployed will fall? Or does it mean simply that because the total number of under-24-year-olds will be lower, the total number of unemployed under-24-year-olds will be lower? If it meant the latter, then it would not be adding to the point made by reason (a), so presumably it means that the percentage of under-24-year-olds who are unemployed will fall. This depends on an assumption that the number of jobs for people in this age group will remain roughly the same, or may increase.

In relation to reason (c), it is assumed that the installation of video cameras in Airdrie and Bournemouth *caused* the reduction in crime; and in relation to reason (e), that neighbourhood watch schemes can contribute to a reduction in crime.

We need to clarify what is meant in reason (f) by saying that the five factors 'ought to have greater impact than each would have individually'. Presumably it doesn't just mean that five (or four, or three, or two) factors will have more impact than one. That would be so obvious as to be hardly worth saying. So what is meant here is that these factors reinforce each other, so that each one of them has greater impact than it would have alone. There is an assumption connected with the two reasons for the second conclusion – that being 'watched' by video cameras, and living in a more censorious society are 'costs'.

3   Let us consider first the truth of reasons relating to the first conclusion. The truth of reason (a) depends on the accuracy of the figures quoted, which could be checked from official sources.

The assumption connected with reason (a) – that there will probably be no increase in crimes committed by groups other than young men – is reasonable if figures generally show that other groups have a fairly low crime rate which has not been rising over recent years.

In relation to reason (b), we might first question whether unemployment rates make a difference to crime. This claim would be reinforced to some extent if figures show that when unemployment rises, so does crime, and that when unemployment falls, so does crime (though this would not necessarily show that there was a causal connection). The remarks made in the passage about unemployment giving a greater amount of time in which to commit crimes give some support to the claim.

The truth of the claim that unemployment might decrease could have been questioned at the time the article was written. It could have been pointed out that the high unemployment of the 1980s may have been due to some extent to modern technology reducing the number of workers needed. This could have suggested that the high unemployment rates in the 1980s, though unusual in relation to the past, may not be unusual in the future.

The assumption connected with reason (b) – that the number of jobs for people in the under-24 age group will not decrease – is likely to be true, provided there is no overall *increase* in unemployment.

It seems reasonable to accept that reason (c) is true, which involves accepting that video cameras deter people from committing crimes, and improve detection rates.

Reason (d) is difficult to evaluate. Perhaps it is true that police performance is improving. It is not clear whether the author is claiming that the police are now preventing more crimes, or that they are detecting and solving more crimes, and thus bringing more criminals to justice. The example used in connection with this relates to crime prevention – the improved behaviour of football fans because of improvements in policing. Perhaps police figures could give some indication as to whether it is true that more crimes are being solved. It is clear that the author thinks that solving more crimes could eventually lead to a reduction in crimes committed, since he says that when detection rates rise, 'crime simply becomes an unattractive proposition'.

To evaluate reason (e), we would need to look for figures which indicate an increase in the numbers of neighbourhood watch schemes. To evaluate the assumption that neighbourhood watch schemes can help to reduce crime, we would need to look at crime figures in comparable areas, some of which have, and some of which do not have, neighbourhood watch schemes; or compare crime rates in one area before the neighbourhood watch scheme was set up with crime rates after it was set up.

Reason (f), and its related assumption, that the five factors reinforce each other is also difficult to evaluate, though it does seem reasonable to claim that if crime comes down as a result of demographic changes, the police will be better able to deal with such crime as there is, and that improvements in detection rates will have a further impact on the amount of crime committed.

Now we must consider the truth of the reasons relating to the second conclusion. The first reason is acceptable. If surveillance cameras are to be used widely in order to deter and catch criminals, then we shall all have to get used to being observed.

The truth of the second reason is less clear. It is not obvious that a greater hostility to crime, and greater organisation against it by the public, will produce a society which is 'more hostile to people who do not conform to what other people regard as normal and proper'. It depends upon whether a clear distinction can be made between crime and non-conforming behaviour.

The truth of the assumption that these developments would be 'costs' is also dubious. No doubt it is true that if people who did not break the law, but merely had unusual lifestyles, were to suffer greater hostility, this would be a 'cost'. But we have challenged the truth of this reason. As for the other reason, it is not obvious that greater surveillance of, for example, shopping areas would be regarded as a cost by the majority of law-abiding citizens.

4   No authorities are mentioned in the passage.

5   Additional evidence might be sought concerning the causes of crime. The passage says little about what causes crime – beyond the comments about the relationship between unemployment and crime. If it were found that the increase in crime was caused by factors still operating in our society (the author does mention a possible link between drugs and crime), then crime could continue to increase, or remain at a high level, despite the factors listed in the passage which, it is claimed, will lead to a decrease in crime.

It is interesting in this section to consider evidence which has come to light since 1994. Shortly after this piece was written, a video was released of footage from a closed-circuit television. It showed members of the public, who were unaware they were being filmed, in situations which they could find embarrassing to have publicly shown. This strengthens the claim that there is some danger to the liberty of individuals when surveillance methods are used. But perhaps this can be dealt with in the way recommended by some critics of the release of this video – by legislation to ensure that cameras are used only for security purposes, and to make it a criminal offence to use such material for entertainment.

Since the article was written, unemployment has fallen, and the crime figures published in January 2001 show that recorded crime has fallen by about 7 per cent since 1997. But despite this overall fall in crime, certain categories of crime – for example, violent crime and robberies – have seen an increase. Drug offences, burglary and car crime have fallen. It has been suggested that some of the increase in violent crime and robberies could be due to changes in the way the police record crimes, and to the willingness of people to report incidents of domestic violence. There have been more street muggings (so either CCTV is not deterring, or is not widespread enough), and a large part of the increase in robberies is attributed to mobile phone thefts by teenagers from teenagers. The fall in car crime may be partly attributable to better theft protection devices, and perhaps the rise in robberies can be accounted for by the fact that there are more items, such as mobile phones, which are easy to steal – something which the writer of this article had not envisaged.

6   A number of explanations are referred to in the passage:

- that the fall in crime in Airdrie and Bournemouth can be explained by the presence of video cameras deterring criminals;
- that better behaviour at football matches is due to better policing; and
- that the fall in crime in Scotland can be attributed to, amongst other things, neighbourhood watch schemes and better co-operation between police and public.

None of these explanations is implausible.

7   No comparisons were identified in the text.

8   No firm conclusions can be drawn from the information in the passage.

9   No parallel arguments come to mind.

10   The argument does not rely on any general principles.

11   The passage presented quite a strong case for believing that the factors identified could, in the absence of factors which might counteract their influence, lead to a reduction in crime. The weakest areas related to unemployment and changes in policing. Unemployment may be linked to high crime rates, but no strong reason was given for believing that unemployment would fall. Unemployment has fallen, perhaps partly due to government policies – contrary to the author's claim that the envisaged reduction in crime has 'nothing to do with politicians'. The remarks about improvements in policing are not given support with concrete evidence.

Negative forces which could counteract the influence of these five factors were mentioned, but the author insisted that because the five factors would reinforce each other, they would be likely to turn round the alarming rise in crime. But it was possible that these 'offsetting negative forces' would be stronger than the author thought; that those who felt 'even more excluded and alienated' would increase their crime rate, and that drug related crime would increase. In the event, drug crime did not increase, but robberies did – perhaps partly due to the unforeseen 'negative force' of more goods to steal from people in the street.

The passage did not make a very strong case for the claim that our society was likely to 'become less exuberant, less interesting, and in some senses, less free' if crime fell. To some extent the strength of the case depends upon how we interpret the word 'free'. It is true that the greater use of surveillance equipment in the attempt to deter criminals restricts our liberty in one respect – that in many public areas we are not free to go about our business unobserved by the police. But if this reduces crime, then perhaps we are more free in another respect.

Summary: Assessing an argument

Analysing	Evaluating
1 Identify conclusion and reasons: • look for 'conclusion indicators', • look for 'reason indicators' and/or • ask 'What is the passage trying to get me to accept or believe?' • ask 'What reasons/evidence is it using in order to get me to believe this?'	3 Evaluate truth of reasons and assumptions: • how would you seek further information in order to help you to do this? 4 Assess the reliability of any authorities on whom the reasoning depends. 5 Is there any additional evidence which strengthens or weakens the conclusion? • anything which may be true? • anything which you know to be true?
2 Identify unstated assumptions: • assumptions supporting basic reasons, • assumptions functioning as additional reasons, assumptions functioning as intermediate conclusions, • assumptions concerning the meanings of words, • assumptions about analogous or comparable situations, • assumptions concerning the appropriateness of a given explanation.	6 Assess the plausibility of any explanation you have identified. 7 Assess the appropriateness of any analogies or comparisons you have identified. 8 Can you draw any conclusions from the passâge? If so, do they suggest that the reasoning in the passage is faulty? 9 Is any of the reasoning in the passage parallel with reasoning which you know to be flawed? 10 Do any of the reasons or assumptions embody a general principle? If so, evaluate it. 11 Is the conclusion well supported by the reasoning? If not, can you state the way in which the move from the reasons to the conclusion is flawed? Use your answers to questions 5 to 10 to help you to do this.

Exercise 20: Ten longer passages to evaluate

Now you can try your hand on the following ten passages. Use the same eleven steps that we used in evaluating the two examples above.

1   Cry-babies and colic

Some mothers suffer agony from incessantly crying babies during the first three months of life. Nothing the parents do seems to stem the flood. They usually conclude that there is something radically, physically wrong with the infants and try to treat them accordingly. They are right, of course, that there is something physically wrong; but it is probably effect rather than cause. The vital clue comes with the fact that this so-called 'colic' crying ceases, as if by magic, around the third or fourth month of life. It vanishes at just the point where the baby is beginning to be able to identify its mother as a known individual.

A comparison of the parental behaviour of mothers with cry babies and those with quieter infants gives the answer. The former are tentative, nervous and anxious in their dealings with their offspring. The latter are deliberate, calm and serene. The point is that even at this tender age, the baby is acutely aware of differences in tactile 'security' and 'safety', on the one hand, and tactile 'insecurity' and 'alarm' on the other. An agitated mother cannot avoid signalling her agitation to her new-born infant. It signals back to her in the appropriate manner, demanding protection from the cause of the agitation. This only serves to increase the mother's distress, which in turn increases the baby's crying. Eventually the wretched infant cries itself sick and its physical pains are then added to the sum total of its already considerable misery.

All that is necessary to break the vicious circle is for the mother to accept the situation and become calm herself. Even if she cannot manage this (and it is almost impossible to fool a baby on this score) the problem corrects itself, as I said, in the third or fourth month of life, because at that stage the baby becomes imprinted on the mother, and instinctively begins to respond to her as the 'protector'. She is no longer a disembodied series of agitating stimuli, but a familiar face. If she continues to give agitating stimuli, they are no longer so alarming because they are coming from a known source with a friendly identity. The baby's growing bond with its parent then calms the mother and automatically reduces her anxiety. The 'colic' disappears.

(Desmond Morris, *The Naked Ape*, New York:
Dell Publishing Co. Inc., 1967, pp. 98–9)

2   The good news is that sport is bad for us

Thomas Sutcliffe

When I was at school I regularly used to be hurled to the ground by boys much larger than myself. My face would be mashed into an icy compound of mud and grit, my shins kicked, and my clothes torn. And the teachers did not merely condone this brutality, they looked on approvingly and yelled incitements until they were red in the face.

This was because somewhere in the vicinity – as far away from me as I could contrive – a slippery oval ball was being fought for with a fury that would give check to an anarchist mob. To add to the general torment, the offal rendering plant located next to the school playing fields ensured that what we sucked into our racked lungs was as distant from good fresh air as was compatible with the languid Health and Safety regulations.

But it wasn't the stench or the physical discomfort I minded most. It wasn't even the scorn and contempt regularly visited on sporting in-adequates. It was the repeated insistence that this unpleasant ordeal was actually morally improving.

So when I say that I greet every new revelation of sporting corrup-tion and malpractice with an inner whoop of glee I hope you'll understand that this isn't simply a demonic exaltation at the triumph of vice. What makes me want to sing and skip is the delicious sound of another nail being hammered into the coffin of a tyrant – the bullying fallacy that sport can tone up the ethical muscles. If it isn't quite dead yet, the notion is surely in a vegetative coma.

On one side the captain of the South African cricket team, a paragon of sportsmanship, admits to lying and is accused of worse. The International Cricket Council meets to inquire into match-fixing. Scottish and Welsh rugby players fudge their ancestry to play on the national teams (your grandfather once bought a bag of Edinburgh rock? Oh, that'll do) and the Tour de France buckles under the weight of illegal drugs. Premier League football clubs strip their supporters of cash like ants milking aphids. Everywhere a landscape of rules broken, corners cut, justice defaced and reputation traded for cash.

You could argue – and they do – that this has nothing to do with sport. What we're seeing, they say, is the canker of money eating into an essentially noble ideal. There are two answers to that. The first is that a true sportsman doesn't need a financial incentive to cheat. Just think of the scandals that regularly erupt in the humble worlds of skittles and pub darts, where there is often nothing more at stake than village pride.

The second is that, if the basic argument has any value at all, sportsmen and women should be even better armoured against temptation than ordinary mortals, annealed by their efforts into a stainless rectitude.

It isn't as if these are complicated or ambiguous rules either – businessmen may justifiably argue that it's sometimes difficult to see when aggressive competition turns into something less reputable, but in sport the sidelines couldn't be more clearly marked.

The truth is, though, that most top sportsmen aren't slightly better people than the rest of us, they're slightly worse – because their definition of 'winning at all costs' will always be broader and more ruthless. And sport rewards ruthlessness since it is a zero-sum game – for someone to win another person must lose. 'Nice guys finish last', as the American baseball coach, Leo Durocher famously put it. Because of this sport will always be morally vulnerable; like water on limestone, money simply finds its natural weakness and inexorably opens it up.

Of course, there are things to be said for sport. Yes, it can provide examples of human transcendence and moments of great beauty. It can even, I have discovered, be fun. But as a moral tutor you'd have to admit it's an absolute loser.

(The Independent, 4 May 2000)

3   Slippery slope of legalising drugs

Professor P. A. J. Waddington

The newly elected leader of the Liberal Democrats has stirred up a storm by suggesting the legalisation of soft drugs should be reviewed by a Royal Commission.

There is a strong argument for legalisation. It is demonstrable that outlawing these drugs has failed to stem, still less eliminate, their sale. All the indications are that the consumption of illicit drugs is now commonplace – especially among the young. So, if we can't beat it, perhaps we should try regulating it. This, after all was surely the lesson to be learned from the American experiment with Prohibition. Outlawing commodities that people want to buy simply encourages criminals to supply them, leading to gangsterism. It also leads otherwise law-abiding people into the clutches of those with a vested interest in ensuring that they become addicted to harder drugs.

Regulation not only eliminates criminal involvement, it can ensure product standards. When people buy illicit drugs they have no idea how strong the dose will turn out to be, with the obvious risk of overdosing. And let me remind those who say 'serves them right', that the victim might easily be a member of their family. Distribution through legitimate retail outlets means the consumption of these drugs would also be controlled through the informal rules that surround any social activity. Pubs dispense a potentially lethal drug in ways that encourage moderate usage. It is hugely watered down, mixed with non-alcoholic beverages, and regarded as an accompaniment to sociability, rather than an end in itself. These are all more effective controls than the threat of police action.

As advocates for the legalisation of cannabis are fond of telling us, the harm that cannabis does is far less than that done by alcohol. They are absolutely correct: the drug problem on university campuses nation-wide is that of alcohol – not cannabis or amphetamines. However, this is precisely where I find the argument for legalisation unconvincing. The regulation of alcohol is held up as a model to emulate and Prohibition as a failure to be avoided. It seems strange to claim that a policy has been a 'success' when it evidently produces such mayhem. The country that has pursued policies of decriminalising soft drug consumption most avidly is, of course, the Netherlands. It has the highest crime rate in the western world in the recently published International Crime Survey. When my wife and I visited Amsterdam, we took the opportunity of revisiting the youth we never had and threw ourselves on the mercy of the propri-etor who sold us a couple of cannabis chocolates. Apart from sending us both soundly and gigglingly to sleep, my experience was that taking dope was very different to consuming alcohol. It was an act of deliberately consuming a drug in order to experience the effect. This is not how I experience the consumption of alcohol, where the effect is almost an incidental by-product of the taste of the wine or beer and conviviality of the circumstances.

The suggestion that the adverse consequences of soft-drug use owes most to the fact that it is outlawed, also seems contrary to experience. In the 1970s and 1980s Scotland suffered particularly from heroin addic-tion. The path that addicts seem to have taken was via solvent abuse. Now, at that time the supply of solvents was both legal and abundant, and their abuse was not outlawed. Yet solvent abuse seemed to be the slippery slope down which many young people tragically slid into heroin addiction.

The 'slippery slope' argument is revealing in another sense: advo-cates of legalisation insist that without the involvement of criminal suppliers cannabis use need not lead to addiction to harder drugs. Implicit in this argument (which some advocates are willing to make quite explicit) is the acceptance that hard drugs should remain illegal. Of course, this raises the whole thorny issue of where the line between 'soft' and 'hard' should be drawn. It is predictable that having legalised cannabis, another campaign would commence to legalise cocaine and heroin.

I don't know where this leaves us, but mine's a pint.

(*Police Review*, 27 August 1999)

4   Scandal schools

A. C. Grayling

The opening of Britain's first state-funded Sikh school this week follows the example of five others – two Jewish, two Muslim and one Seventh Day Adventist – which have abandoned independence for the shelter of state funding since Labour came to power. They join long-established Anglican and Roman Catholic schools in getting public money for inculcating their own brand of belief in their students.

Labour is more responsive to the claims of 'minority faiths' than the last Conservative government and has responded sympathetically to their concerns. In the reformed House of Lords, bishops are to be joined by equivalents from other faiths. Jack Straw has been listening to the arguments of leaders of the British Muslim community for extension of legal protections against Islamophobia. Spokesmen for the religions rightly argue that it is inappropriate to claim protection under race legislation, because their faiths can embrace many different ethnicities. That makes it harder to defend themselves when their dress or behaviour comes into conflict with mainstream British life.

All of these signs of government sympathy must be encouraging to people of a religious persuasion. To anyone who is not religious, they are troublingly misguided.

Discrimination against any individual on any ground of race, creed, or sexual orientation is wrong, and any individual must be allowed to believe, or to do in private, whatever he or she likes, providing it does no harm to others. (This view is far more liberal than most religious practitioners would like; the consideration they seek for themselves they tend not to extend to sexual orientation.)

But these vitally important principles apply only to individuals, not to groups. It would be impossible to carry an argument to the effect that, say, paid-up members of the Conservative party, considered as an identifiable group, have rights by virtue of their group membership: for example, to be protected from sarcastic remarks or scorn, or the taking of their leader's name in vain.

To think in terms of groups is precisely the fault of the racist or snob: he discriminates against another because of the group he thinks the other belongs to, thereby failing to accord him his rights as an individual. Group thinking is the problem, not the solution, in matters of human rights.

Suppose a group forms around the belief that there are UFOs which will one day save mankind. Are they to get extra protections as a result, and perhaps state funding for a school in which children can be raised in unshakeable beliefs about UFOs?

There is nowhere to draw a line between 'responsible' religions and unfounded superstitions. For that reason, what people privately choose to believe cannot be a ground for them to get extra consideration when they band together.

It is certainly an anomaly that Christianity is protected in Britain by laws, for example against blasphemy, whereas other faiths are not. The remedy is not to extend such laws to other religions, but to abandon them altogether, and to disestablish the Church.

On a plain interpretation of what each religion orthodoxly believes, Christianity and Islam mutually blaspheme each other, the former because it does not accept the Prophet, and the latter because it denies the Holy Ghost. If both faiths were legally protected against blasphemy, it would be open to litigious enthusiasts in either cause to make money for the lawyers.

Problems will also arise, for example, over female circumcision and the rights of women generally. Most minority faiths seeking protection for their ways of life in contemporary Britain have attitudes and practices regarding women which are in conflict with the mainstream, and the differences are deep and important.

Religion is a matter of private persuasion. For a secularist such as myself, it is a matter for regret that people should live by false or absurd beliefs, and a matter of scandal that they should indoctrinate their children, yet incapable of thinking for themselves.

The thought that public money – my taxes included – should go to support any group of people, Christian or otherwise, in doing so, adds to the scandal. Religious schools, if they are to exist at all, should be privately funded affairs, and allowing them to move from the independent to the maintained sector is wrong.

No organised religions wish to concede the principle that faith is a matter of individual decision, because without discipline, community pressure, and especially indoctrination of children, they would all quickly evaporate, leaving an unreflective chaos of vague new age-type beliefs such as now exist among the post-Christian majority of the mainstream.

Most of these superstitions are too unsystematic and weakly held to produce fanatics and fundamentalists, which all of the organised religions possess on their fringes; and they are likewise too unsystematic to claim funding or legal protection for their crystal-rubbing or pendulum-wearing activities. That is how it should be for all kinds of faith, however ancient or well-organised they might now be.

(*The Guardian*, 1 December 1999)

5 Goodness and greed

However noisy the demonstrations against global capitalism, ethics in business are unenforceable

Frances Cairncross

'Smash capitalism', announced the banners of the protesters in the Washington streets last weekend. Global capitalism has a bad name these days, even when it takes the form of such innocuous British giants as Unilever, currently being reviled on American websites for buying Ben & Jerry's, makers of fashionable ice cream. So perhaps it is not surprising that more and more companies want to be seen to be good. They set up advisory committees on social responsibility; they write codes of corporate ethics; they appoint ethics officers; they talk of their duties to their stakeholders. Admirable though such efforts may appear, they are founded on a moral misunderstanding.

Companies that strive to behave ethically generally argue that they do so because, in the long run, it is good for business. Most of the time they are right. Sometimes, indeed, they have little option, because ethical behaviour is what the law demands. In most countries, at least in the rich world, the law discourages companies from lying to customers, cheating their employees, or stealing from taxpayers. The primary moral duties of those who run companies are to obey the law, and to ensure that their employees do too.

Good behaviour may spring from other self-interested motives. For instance, in the United States various laws and court rulings encourage managers to tell employees how to behave ethically and to see that they do so. In addition, it has become more embarrassing to be caught doing something unethical. Non-governmental organisations fight hard for members and money these days; and they gain good publicity from harrying a company caught doing something questionable. As Shell and Nike can ruefully attest, being blitzed by NGOs is bad for staff morale, brand strength and the management self-confidence.

More fundamentally, a reputation for ethical behaviour may be a competitive advantage. A firm such as Hewlett Packard would argue that it treats employees, suppliers and customers well because to do so attracts good staff, ensures good service and enhances the value of its brands. Trust is valuable – and will grow more so in an electronic world, where buyers and sellers may be geographically far apart.

Such arguments allow companies to say that they are combining virtue with the pursuit of shareholder value. But what happens when virtue and value clash? Many executives would argue that corporate decisions are rarely black or white.

Say a mining company has a joint venture with a state-owned enterprise in a developing country, which does not care about western safety or environmental standards. Does it pull out, knowing that it might be replaced by another company with fewer scruples, or stay put and try to change things?

Yet every executive, every corporate board, at some point faces a decision that does not quite pass the smell test. A drug company offers health officials from developing countries lavish entertainment as an inducement to buy its drugs. A bank tries to coax people on modest incomes to borrow money to pay for holidays. An internet company sells information gleaned about its customers' surfing habits without their consent. In each case, the company's managers can reasonably argue that they are pursuing the interests of shareholders, and not breaking the law. Is this wrong?

The question makes it clear why corporate ethics is such a tangle. It is hard to think of companies as moral entities, on a par with human beings. A company has, as someone once said, 'No soul to damn, no backside to kick'. It may have legal obligations that apply to it as an organisation; but it cannot do good or bad without action by the individuals who work for it and own it. In some companies the corporate culture may be so powerful that it appears to infuse the whole business with a sense of moral values; in others, anything goes. But, while the corporate culture may make it easier or harder for people to behave well, it does not mean that the company has an independent moral existence.

Indeed, ethical codes – the real sort, rather than the kind consultants are paid to concoct – are simply too complex and subtle to be applied to companies. This is not merely because moral values are hard to agree upon: who knows what is 'fair pay', or whether pension schemes should treat same-sex couples as though they were married? It is also because companies cannot love their neighbours, or forgive those that hate them, or even act altruistically. These basic moral tasks are human, not corporate.

Where, then, does that leave the individual manager, torn between his corporate responsibility to shareholders and his conscience?

The moral manager applies two tests to any difficult decision. First, how would this look if it were to appear on the front page of a newspaper? And second, will he still be able to look himself in the mirror tomorrow morning without a twinge?

Because companies cannot ask the second question, it is the one that ultimately determines what corporate ethics means.

(© Frances Cairncross, *The Guardian*, 21 April 2000)

6 We should recycle the dead to help the living

John Harris

There is a crisis in organ donation. In the UK, around 5,000 people a year need kidneys alone, and there are fewer than half the number of donors registered to meet the demand. Worse, 30 per cent of relatives of people who have died refuse to allow organs to be used. This means that many hundreds of people are dying every year for want of donor organs in the UK alone. World-wide, it is a major problem with 50,000 people waiting for organs in the US and 70,000 in India.

The donor card scheme is clearly failing us all. We must get away from the idea that people can allow their bodies and those of their relatives to be simply buried or burned when they die. This is a terrible and cruel waste of organs and tissue that may save life or restore health.

The problem is that we, as a society, have leant over backwards to make sure that potential donors and their relatives are protected against anything that might cause them distress or unease. But the same consideration has not been shown to potential organ recipients and their families. Both are entitled to our concern. There are then two groups of people we must consider: donors and recipients. If we ask what each group stands to lose if their preferences are not respected, we get very different answers. One group stands to lose their lives. The other group has already lost theirs and, at worst, will know prior to death that one of the many things they want will not come to pass.

One way of expressing an equality of concern for both groups of people, bearing in mind what both stand to lose, would be to ensure, through legislation, that all organs from dead bodies should be automatically available at death without any consent being required. The dead, after all, have no further use for their organs; the living do.

Such a proposal, if accepted, would have many advantages. It would mean that virtually all cadaver organs were automatically available and doctors would not have to ask dying people if they consent to their organs being used. Neither would they have to ask grieving relatives such a difficult question at perhaps the worst possible moment.

People think that there would be many religious objections to such a simple proposal. This seems doubtful since there has never been an outcry against the present system in which coroners may order post-mortem examinations of the dead without any consent being required. No one may opt out and there is no provision for conscientious objection. Moreover, as is now well known, organs are often removed during such examinations and not replaced. We have all accepted that there is an important public interest at stake here. It matters very much both that murders do not go undetected and that illnesses and accidents that cause death be properly understood so that others may be protected. There is a clear and important public interest here. But how much more so in the case of organ donation. Organs are required to save life, not merely to explain suspicious deaths. If there is a public interest in the one case, there is surely also a strong public interest in providing donor organs to save lives.

Some fears have been expressed that if organs can be automatically used, doctors may have less incentive to strive to keep people alive if there are people waiting to receive organs. There are two important things to note about such fears. The first is that there is absolutely no evidence that people who currently carry donor cards have ever been given anything other than the best possible care because they are eligible as donors. But perhaps even more crucial — if people are worried about their chances of survival — is the fact that they are more likely at the moment to need an organ and not get it than to be ill and not properly treated. So prudential self-interest also supports the automatic availability of cadaver organs.

Some people will have strong objections to their bodies being tampered with after death. Some of their objections will be based on religious belief or cultural practice. Any decent society will try hard to accommodate genuine conscientious objection to whatever practice. Since people with strong, enduring and conscience based objections to cadaver transplants are likely to be few, it is almost certain that we can accommodate such views and still save the lives of all those who are dying for want of donor organs.

The crunch, of course, comes when this is not the case and conscientious objection will cost lives. Then we have a hard choice to make. It is surely far from clear that people are entitled to conscientiously object to practices that will save innocent lives. However, if we make sure that conscientious objection really is just that, and apply tests comparable to those for people who claim conscientious exemption from military service in time of war, it is likely that the exceptions will be sufficiently few for such hard choices to be avoided. We may note that there is no provision, so far as I am aware, for conscientious objection to compulsory post-mortem examinations.

Fully consensual schemes are always best. But when so much is at stake, we must consider even mandatory schemes. The scheme that I have proposed will save lives, and the costs, while significant, are not incompatible with the values of a decent democratic society – as coroner ordered post-mortem examinations demonstrate.

(*The Independent*, 19 February 1999)

7 The following passage concerns the trial of Greenpeace members accused of causing criminal damage in relation to their destruction of a field of genetically modified crops. The defence argued that their actions did not constitute criminal damage, because the damage they admittedly and deliberately caused was aimed at preventing greater damage to the environment which would be caused by allowing GM crops to continue to grow. A jury found them not guilty.

They were wrong

Greenpeace's action was vandalism and inhibited the need for scientific research

Richard Dawkins

Defence counsel for the Greenpeace vandals reassured the court that his clients were 'the sort of people you may expect to find sitting on a jury'.

He was right, of course, with a vengeance. But far from being a character reference for the defendants, it is an indictment of the jury system. I am not in the least surprised to read that after the trial members of the jury were seen 'congratulating defendants'.

What sort of signal has been sent out by this verdict? Is it, as some have said, a charter for burglars, arsonists and telephone box vandals? Can we now freely commit crimes on the assumption that a jury of Big Brother-watching *Sun* readers will reach a verdict uncontaminated by the facts of the case? It hasn't quite come to that. But it is close. This, emphatically, is not to be compared with the sort of civil disobedience that can be justified on genuinely thoughtful grounds.

Lord Melchett is no Gandhi, no Mandela, taking direct action as the only possible recourse against an oppressive regime. On the other hand he and his friends are probably not as sinister as their 'decontamination suit' uniforms suggest. On balance, Lord Melchett is more airheaded wally than Mosleyite stormtrooper.

The air force general in Dr Strangelove who took devastating direct action in defence of 'our precious bodily fluids', is fiction . . . just. Popular misconceptions about GM foods are well up in the 'precious bodily fluids' class. If you pick 12 people at random, the majority might well think that GM is a substance, like DDT. Or that if they are 'contaminated' by GM they will undergo some Frankensteinian transmogrification. Or they wouldn't understand what is funny about the protesters' slogan: 'We don't want DNA in our tomatoes'. Aren't there some beliefs too daft for 'sincerity' to be an excuse?

Many of us believe the *News of the World* is an affront to decent humanity. Are we now free to torch its editorial offices? Many people sincerely think abortion is legalised murder. Will the Greenpeace verdict signal open season on doctors and clinics, as happens in some parts of America?

Some people sincerely believe that their private opinions on petrol prices entitle them to take unilateral action and blockade the country's vital supplies. Presumably, Greenpeace would oppose them, since high petrol taxes help to reduce pollution. We don't have to project our imaginations far into the future to envision Greenpeace warriors storming the barricades of fuel-protesting lorry drivers. If there are casualties and damage, should the jury acquit both sides, on the grounds that both sincerely believed their (opposite and incompatible) doctrines?

Is this really the sort of country we want to live in? Is this how we want to decide policy? That is where the Greenpeace verdict seems to be leading us.

The Government may be ruefully wondering whether it has been hoist by its own petard. Was it wise to encourage those outbursts of mindless 'feeling' and all that hysterical caterwauling over the 'People's Princess'? Has feeling become the new thinking? If so, the Government may bear some indirect responsibility.

The late Carl Sagan was once asked a question to which he didn't know the answer and he firmly said so. The questioner persisted: 'But what is your gut feeling?' Sagan's reply is never to be forgotten: 'But I try not to think with my gut. If I'm serious about understanding the world, thinking with anything besides my brain, as tempting as that might be, is likely to get me into trouble. It's OK to reserve judgment until the evidence is in.'

I genuinely don't know what to think about genetically modified crops, and nor should anyone else. The evidence is not yet in. Particular kinds of genetic modification may be a very bad idea. Or they may be a very good idea. It is precisely because we don't know that we have to find out. That is the purpose of experimental trials such as the one sabotaged by Greenpeace. Scientists do not know all the answers and should not claim to. Science is not a testament of doctrines; rather, it is a method of finding out. It is the only method that works by definition, since if a better method comes along, science will incorporate it. If we are not allowed to do experimental trials on genetically modified crops, we shall never know the bad things or the good things about them.

We now know that strong doses of X-rays are very dangerous. They can induce mutations and cause cancers. But if used carefully and in moderation, X-rays are a priceless diagnostic tool. We can all be thankful that predecessor of Greenpeace did not sabotage Roentgen's experiments on X-rays or Muller's investigations of mutagenesis.

We depend on scientific research to predict both the good and bad consequences of innovation. It is a reasonable guess (not a gut feeling) that genetically modified crops will also turn out to have both bad and good aspects. Certainly it will be possible to modify plants to our benefit. And certainly it would be possible to modify plants in deliberately malevolent directions.

Very likely, as in the case of X-rays, even the good modifications may turn out to have some bad side-effects. It would be better to discover these now, in carefully controlled trials, rather than let them emerge later. With hindsight, it is a pity more research was not done earlier on the dangers of X-rays. If it had been, children of my generation would not have been allowed to play with X-ray machines in shoe shops.

We need more research, not less. And if we are to have activists protesting about dangerous crops, let us draw their zealous attention to those crops whose evil effects are already known because the necessary research was allowed to be done. Like tobacco.

(© Richard Dawkins, *The Observer*, 24 September 2000)

8 We could manage without the Net but we will always need shampoo

Hamish McRae

It is, as someone else said in a rather different context, a funny old world. This week we have two global corporate titans, Ford and Unilever, announce that they are getting rid of thousands of their workers. But we are undoubtedly going to go on needing Unilever's washing powder, shampoo and frozen peas, and we will certainly be driving around in Ford cars for another generation. The old economy may be out of fashion, but we still need the things it produces.

Meanwhile the shares of companies like Nokia and Freeserve continue to dazzle. Yet in another 30 years' time the Internet is going to be so utterly different that the companies involved in it may not even exist, and while I do think we will still be making mobile phone calls, surely there won't be much added value in transporting electronic signals across the ether. Put another way, we all could manage without high-speed Internet access, but most of us would find it tough to manage without shampoo.

For personal investors this common sense approach clearly rings true. There is a new boom in people investing on-line, but despite the fact that the dealing is done over the Internet, apparently most of the funds are going into old economy companies.

For professionals in the financial markets, though, high-technology is the only thing that matters. Were it not for a couple of sectors such as mobile communications and any form of Internet-related business, we would be in a bear market, with shares of the old-economy companies plunging almost by the day.

So the professionals have, so far at least, been right. But has the world gone mad? Of course the investment experts in the City and the other financial centres can produce sound arguments to justify this twist in share prices: reasons why those of the old economy should plunge and those of the new should soar. They are very good at it. But all people, however highly paid, make errors of judgement. In the 1980s most of the professionals assumed that the Japanese economy would continue to conquer and that the American one was set for inevitable decline. Now we know that both ideas were rubbish.

So will the current adulation of the new economy look equally daft ten years from now? The answer, I think, is no and yes.

No, because the whole world economy will be transformed in a way that none of us have experienced in our lifetimes. The best analogy, as it happens, is Henry Ford's invention of the production line. This popularised the car, turning it from an elite item into a mass consumer one. Expect a similar transformation to take place as a result of the telecommunications revolution. Just as the production line brought costs down and improved quality, expect a similar change as a result of the Internet.

It is that squeeze on both prices and costs that is spooking the shares of the companies in the old economy. Yes, we will go on shopping in supermarkets, but we will be able to compare prices between them at a click of the mouse. So they have to cut their margins.

But these companies do have a way of fighting back, which is to use the same technology to cut their own costs. We think of [the] communications revolution as chatting to our friends on a mobile or sending e-mails. But the same technology is being used by companies to crunch their production chains. Ordering and paying for components becomes automatic.

An example. A few weeks ago the first generation of hi-tech fridges were rolled out. Apparently they remember if you are running out of, say, milk, and will order more – over a mobile phone – from the supermarket, so that the next delivery will include the appropriate number of cartons.

Now though our stock control at home leaves [a] great deal to be desired, I cannot imagine anything I would like less than have the fridge deciding what to buy from the supermarket. But if you are making shampoo it would presumably be great if the machine always made sure it had the appropriate amount of raw materials. So the Tescos, Unilevers and Fords of the world will spend the next ten years using this new technology to squeeze down costs. Estimates vary, but it is quite plausible that ten years from now the price we pay for goods will be five percentage points lower than it would otherwise be, simply as a result of the new technologies.

But we are not going to wash our hair more often or eat more frozen peas, so volumes will not rise much. It is tough to run a business in a world where prices come down and volumes don't rise. The old economy will be a cold economy.

On the other hand we will make more mobile phone calls – and even if we don't, our children will. More importantly, all the old-economy companies will have to buy expensive communications kit to upgrade their offices and factories. The companies that develop these, the new economy companies, will duly flourish.

At some stage even these new technologies will become common-place. Instead of being the hottest product in town, the web-enabled mobile phone will become just another thing we all have, like a colour television. But there is perhaps another twenty or thirty years before that happens. Meanwhile the boom will continue.

So it is easy to understand the adulation of the new economy, and the concern about the old one. But at the same time, might this adula-tion appear daft a decade from now? Because it has gone too far. There is a long history of markets (and remember that markets are just a collec-tion of individuals) getting carried away with themselves when a new technology bursts out. There were successive railway booms in the last century. There was a radio boom in the US in the 1920s.

During such booms people correctly identify the growth potential of the new technology, but they price it wrongly. Yes, mobile phone pene-tration in Britain will rise from fifty per cent this year to eighty per cent in 2003. But maybe we won't all change our phones every eighteen months as we do now. Maybe phone charges will plunge so much that while we will talk more, we will pay less for the privilege. Suddenly the potential of high-technology firms will be reassessed and, who knows, maybe even the new dot.com companies will have to make a profit.

(*The Independent*, 24 February 2000)

9   Getting to the heart of the matter

Drinking red wine will help you live longer?
This is a fallacy, says Thomas Barlow

Red wine is good for you. It confers protection against heart disease and makes you live longer. Right?

It's funny how a story like that catches on, multiplies, and is never corrected. I don't hold out much hope that what I am about to say will have much effect, but I am determined to knock red wine off its pedestal. So, here goes.

Most people justify the benefits of red wine using an argument based on French statistics. This runs as follows.

Deaths from heart disease are three to four times lower in France than they are in Britain. Yet known risk factors such as smoking levels, and fat or cholesterol consumption are similar in the two countries. (In fact, French fat consumption patterns are very similar to those in the US.)

The French, however, consume much more alcohol than the British. And, in particular, they drink a lot of red wine – which everyone now knows is full of anti-oxidants. Therefore, runs the argument, it must be red wine that is reducing the French incidence of heart disease.

Unfortunately, there is very little epidemiological evidence to support the red wine theory – charming as it must be to red wine producers.

Over the past two decades, there have been a number of longitudinal studies on the effects of alcohol on health. Such studies are fraught with difficulty.

For example, in some early studies, the non-drinkers were actually ex-drinkers who had given up because they were ill. (This is an effect that, in early studies of smokers, appeared to bias 'non-smokers' to high levels of mortality.)

Moreover, the correlation between drinking habits and lifestyle – which includes diet, smoking and exercise levels – can also confound the issue.

However, from the available evidence (and there is now quite a lot), it does seem that one or two alcoholic drinks per day can reduce the risk of heart disease by about 20 per cent. What is not the case is that red wine confers any special advantage not also conferred by white wine, spirits or beer.

This was first demonstrated in studies which compared those who drank only red wine with those who drank only white wine; but recent comparisons of red wine and beer drinkers have led to the same conclusions.

What does sometimes differ between drinkers with a taste for a different tipple is their drinking pattern. For example, beer and spirit drinkers are more likely to drink heavily once or twice a week, whereas wine drinkers may tend to spread out their consumption.

It seems that alcohol protects against heart disease by preventing the formation of blood clots. Since the thinning effects of alcohol on the blood are thought to last less than 24 hours, drinkers who take a small amount each day are more likely to benefit than those who take a lot at once.

When this is taken into account there is no difference in the relative benefits of drinking different tipples.

(And anyone who is younger than their mid-40s, and therefore at low risk of heart disease will probably not benefit from alcohol at all — at least in this sense.) Moreover, this is confirmed at a physiological level. Little difference has been detected between blood samples in people who have imbibed the same amount of alcohol but in different forms.

Rather, the positive effects of the alcohol itself — a shifted balance of cholesterol among the different constituents of the blood, and a reduced likelihood of blood aggregation — are common to all drinks. Certainly, no one has yet found evidence that the fabled anti-oxidant phenolic compounds present in red wine actually increase in the bloodstream with the amount of red wine drunk.

So, it's halfway down from its pedestal. Red wine is only as good for you as beer. But it is possible to go further than this. After all, every gem of epidemiologically based advice comes with a handful of caveats — and there is much more to death than heart disease.

The first caveat is that alcohol (including red wine) is not so good in sub-Saharan Africa. For every man who dies there from heart disease, two will die a violent death. And in this situation, it seems that red wine consumption will not stop you being murdered.

The second caveat is that alcohol (once again, including red wine) is not so beneficial for women as it is for men.

In part, this is because women have a lower risk of heart disease to start with. But it is also because the risks of drinking increase faster for women than they do for men.

For instance, women have a greater susceptibility to liver damage; and the risk of breast cancer in women increases by about 10 per cent for each additional drink per day. (Which may make you wonder, is a woman who drinks red wine for medicinal purposes making a trade-off of one disease for another?)

The third caveat is that alcohol (still including red wine) is not necessarily beneficial for French men either.

The rate of death from heart disease in the UK may be three times that of France. But the rate of deaths from alcohol-related causes (including cancer of the mouth, cirrhosis of the liver and alcohol-related motor vehicle accidents) is three times higher in France than it is in the UK.

(And, incidentally, in the UK, where alcohol consumption is rising, the death rate from cirrhosis of the liver is also increasing.)

That's probably all we need to know about red wine. But what about France? If there is nothing especially protective about red wine, what's special about France? Why do the French have such a low incidence of heart disease?

Earlier this year, in the *British Medical Journal*, Malcolm Law and Nicholas Wald, epidemiologists at the Wolfson Institute of Preventative Medicine at St. Bartholomew's Hospital in London, published an alternative explanation to the red wine hypothesis.

'In France, the greater alcohol consumption is caused by more drinks per drinker rather than more drinkers. And all alcohol products protect against heart disease, but maximally at one to two units per day', says Law. So the greater alcohol consumption of the French is not giving them any extra protection.

So what has? According to their analysis, it is the effect of time-lag. The discrepancy exists simply because the French diet has been changing and it takes decades of eating a high-fat, high-cholesterol diet for your arteries to firm up.

'Although French fat consumption now is similar to that in America, the high level is relatively recent. They haven't been eating it for as long,' says Law.

Red wine has nothing to do with it.

(*The Financial Times*, weekend
10/11 July 1999)

10   The following article concerns a legal ruling as to whether to separate Siamese twins, both of whom would die if they were not separated, but only one of whom could be saved if they were. The court decided that the twins should be separated, the operation took place, and, as was expected, 'Mary' died and 'Jodie' survived.

The law cannot be a killer – it must save one twin

Melanie Phillips

Solomon himself might have thrown in the towel. It is small wonder that the appeal court judges who are hearing the case of the Siamese twins Jodie and Mary are having sleepless nights.

Separating the month-old twins means Jodie will almost certainly live and probably lead a normal life, although she may be handicapped. Mary, however, will die if she is detached from Jodie. Without separation, both will die within six months.

The twins' parents, who are devout Catholics from a remote Mediterranean community, do not want them separated. They say they cannot kill one daughter to allow the other to live and that nature should take its course.

In the High Court, Mr Justice Johnson ruled, after much agonising, that the twins should be separated. For Lord Justice Ward in the appeal court, this means saying 'save Jodie but murder Mary'. But is that stark and dreadful proposition really the choice that the judges face?

To murder Mary means that she is now alive; but is she? Is she even a separate person? It is not just a matter here of conjoined bodies and shared organs. The image Jodie and Mary call to mind is that of a royal playing card with a head at each end and bodies seamlessly merging into each other. No wonder Lord Justice Brooke was so disturbed by the photograph of what he called 'this creature'. Since it was impossible to say where one baby stopped and the other started, he asked, how could they be separated?

There is surely a yet more pertinent question. Even if Mary is in some fashion a separate individual, is she independently alive? For she has no effective heart, lungs or brain and exists only by using Jodie's oxygenated blood. A baby is born alive if it breathes; if not, we consider it a stillbirth. Mary has never breathed.

The reason she will die if separated is that the only functioning heart and lungs between them belong to Jodie, who is acting as a kind of natural version of a ventilating machine for Mary. So just as dead people may appear to be alive when they are hooked up to an artificial ventilator, Mary's 'life' is merely a simulacrum.

Indeed, to turn Brooke's argument on its head, this is one viable individual, Jodie, whose heart, lungs and brain are functioning, and an only partially formed person to whom she is attached.

Moreover, as was suggested in court, in law Mary might actually be assaulting Jodie, since she is using her organs and thus causing her to die. In other words, refusing to separate them does not mean nature taking its course. It means standing back and doing nothing while one individual inadvertently causes another's death.

A crucial additional point is this: murder means intending to kill. Yet the purpose of the proposed separation is not to kill Mary. It is intended instead to save Jodie. Mary will certainly die as a result; but there is a vital difference between intending to kill Mary, and carrying out a procedure to save Jodie's life that will have the foreseen but unintended consequence of ending Mary's 'life'.

Suppose two people were drowning, one of whom was also fatally injured and was being kept afloat only by the other; and suppose a rescuer could not bring both ashore. Should he really leave both to die so as not to accelerate the death of the one who is already doomed? And by rescuing the one who will survive, is he thus murdering the other? Of course not. In morality, intention is vital.

What is more, is it really in Mary's best interests to be left joined to Jodie? Mary will die whatever happens; indeed, her cells are already dying. As Johnson realised, Mary may be dragged around by Jodie, unable to cry or express her pain in any way. Surely medicine must ensure that Mary dies with no more suffering rather than endure, as one doctor called it, the 'horrendous scenario' of such an awful death?

Into this complex and deeply fraught set of questions intrudes the curious attitude of the Roman Catholic Church. Cormac Murphy-O'Connor, the Archbishop of Westminster, has warned against setting the dangerous precedent that it is lawful to kill a person so that good can come of it. So where does that leave the concept of the 'just war', or the plots in Nazi Germany to kill Hitler?

And where does condemning Jodie to death leave the Catholic belief in the sanctity of life? Cardinal Thomas Winning, the leader of Scotland's Catholics, for once seemed to sit on the fence by saying that both separating and not separating could be morally right. However, he added that the twins should instead be 'kept stable' in Italy under the protection of the Vatican; in other words, a death sentence for Jodie, but without the courage to spell it out.

The alliances in this case are even more curious. The Vatican finds itself supported by the right-to-choose abortion lobby. Yet Baroness Warnock, who herself undermined the sanctity of human existence by recommending that experiments on embryos be made lawful, is lining up with those who think it is important to save Jodie's life. So in this case, extraordinarily, Warnock is more pro-life than her old adversaries the Catholics.

As she says, while the wishes of religious parents are important, they cannot trump the overriding interests of a child. The twins' parents say their superstitious and primitive community will neither understand nor be able to provide for a handicapped baby. What do the 'pro-life' Catholics say to that?

What, indeed, do they say to the distinctly eugenic argument that has been advanced by some of their unlikely bedfellows in this case: that Jodie's life is not worth saving because she will probably be handicapped? Or the ugly fact that the doctors involved have asked to remain anonymous as they fear persecution by zealots whose campaign against infant 'murder' so easily tips into hysteria?

Among both religious and secular folk, therefore, confusion abounds. Science has left us rudderless. We no longer seem to know when life starts, what it is, whether it has intrinsic value, when it ends. Instead, we invent arbitrary definitions for our own convenience.

We also cannot grasp crucial moral distinctions based on intention. Johnson unfortunately used the law lords' decision about Tony Bland, the persistent vegetative state sufferer whose feeding tubes were disconnected, to support his ruling that the twins should be separated. But it was not only the analogy he drew with that case which was unsupportable.

The Bland judgement was an appalling watershed that – ironically – really did make intentional killing lawful. Yet the judges have never grasped this because so few of them seem to understand the key role of intention in moral decisions.

What the judges say in the Siamese twins' case is crucial – not only for their decision but also for the reasons they give. It is not just that they might bring about the death of a baby who otherwise would live. In going the other way, they may lay down a judicial justification for killing, when what is needed instead is a reaffirmation of the duty to preserve life.

Whatever they decide, it is a tragedy for the parents, whose anguish can hardly be imagined.

(© Melanie Phillips/Times Newspapers Limited,
The Sunday Times, 10 September 2000)

Answers to Exercise 20 are given on pp. 186–203.

Exercise 21: Topics for constructing your own arguments

Now that you have worked through the analysis and evaluation of other people's reasoning, you should be confident that you can construct good arguments of your own. Here are some suggestions of topics on which you can put your well-developed skills into practice.

1   Write an argument either in favour of or against single-sex schools.

2   Write an argument in favour of improving and extending rail services in Britain.

3 Write an argument either in favour of or against legalising soft drugs.

4 Write a passage about the benefits and disadvantages of our widespread use of the motor car. Come to a conclusion as to whether the motor car is a good thing or a bad thing.

5 Write an argument about the role, if any, that families could play in reducing crime.

6 Write an argument either in favour of or against restrictions of the freedom of the press to write about the lives of individuals.

7 Write an argument about whether the monarchy in Britain is a good thing.

8 Write an argument about whether capital punishment should be reintroduced in Britain.

9 Write an argument about the use of animals in medical research.

10 Write an argument either for or against the idea of a 'right' to have children.

Answers to exercises

Exercise 1: Identifying arguments and conclusions

1   This is an argument, and the conclusion is the first sentence. The evidence that those who have pets are less likely to suffer from depression and high blood pressure gives a reason to support the claim that pets are good for you, provided we can assume that it is the presence of the pet which accounts for the benefit to health. To rewrite the passage, reverse the order of the two sentences, and insert 'so' or 'therefore' before the claim that 'pets are good for you'.

2   This is not an argument. It makes three statements about animals and disease, none of which gives any support to the others. The third sentence is clearly unconnected with the other two, since it is about diseases carried by rabbits, whereas the other two are about a disease carried by cats. But neither of the first two sentences supports the other. They simply report two facts about the disease which cats carry – that it can cause miscarriages to pregnant women, and that most cat owners are probably immune to it.

3   This is not an argument. It gives information about good spellers and poor spellers, but none of these claims follows from any of the others. The two claims about poor spellers are not supported by the information about good spellers, and there is no obvious connection between the two claims about poor spellers.

4   This is an argument, and the conclusion is the second sentence. The word 'should' in this sentence indicates that a recommendation is being made to compensate farmers for taking riverside farmland out of production. The rest of the passage provides the reasons for this – that it would save money and benefit the environment. The passage can be rewritten as follows:

> Millions of pounds of public money are spent defending riverside farm-land from flooding. Some of this money could be given to farmers to compensate them for taking such land out of production. This would save money and would benefit the environment, since if rivers were allowed to flood, their natural flood plains would provide wetland meadows and wood-land rich in wildlife. So some of the money spent on defending riverside farmland from flooding should be given to farmers to compensate them for taking such land out of production.

5   This is not an argument. It simply reports some items of information about the weather.

6   This is an argument, and the conclusion is the final sentence. Notice that this sentence begins with the phrase 'This indicates', suggesting that a conclusion is being drawn from the evidence about increases in sightings of bald eagles. The conclusion also relies on the assumption (not explicitly stated) that if there has been an increase in sightings, there must be more eagles. To rewrite the passage, simply insert 'So' before the last sentence.

7   This is an argument, and the conclusion is that security cameras are not an unqualified success. The passage could be rewritten as follows:

> The presence of security cameras has been shown to reduce crime in areas such as shopping malls. However, law-abiding citizens do not wish to have all their activities observed, and criminals may commit just as much crime, but do so in areas where there are no cameras. So security cameras are not an unqualified success.

8   This is an argument. It may be more difficult to see this than with other examples, because the conclusion is not set out in a simple sentence. Yet there clearly is some reasoning going on, and a recommendation is being made that we should not lower speed limits in order to deal with the problem of unsafe drivers. The reason given for this is that to do so would incon-venience the majority who drive safely. The passage could be rewritten as follows:

Although we could reduce road accidents by lowering speed limits, and making greater efforts to ensure that such limits are enforced, this would inconvenience the majority who drive safely. Therefore, it would be an unacceptable solution to the problem of careless drivers who are unsafe at current speed limits.

9   This is not an argument. It simply gives three pieces of information about cannabis – that in the Victorian era it was used to treat various conditions, that now its use is illegal, and that it can relieve the symptoms of multiple sclerosis. None of these gives support to any of the others.

10   This is an argument, and the conclusion is the last sentence. The word 'thus' in this sentence indicates that a conclusion is being drawn. Although 'thus' appears in the first sentence also, it is not introducing a main conclusion here, but playing a part in the reasoning of the social historians with whom the main conclusion is going to disagree. The word 'however' signals the introduction of disagreement, and is followed by the reasons which give support to the main conclusion.

Exercise 3: Identifying reasons

1   The answer is (c).
    (c) supports the recommendation to pay blood donors by mentioning an advantage of doing so – that it would remedy or reduce the shortage of blood donors by encouraging more people to become donors.
    (a) does not support the conclusion, because it suggests that the Blood Donor service may not be able to afford to pay donors.
    (b) may look tempting, but it does not support the conclusion, unless we assume that people should always be paid for helping others. It suggests that for many people, there is no *need* to pay them in order to motivate them to give blood.

2   The answer is (b).
    (b) supports the conclusion since if employers ignore the importance of applicants' personalities, they may appoint someone with an unsuitable personality which cannot be changed. If, however, they appoint someone with a suitable personality, they can easily teach this person the necessary skills.
    (a) does not support the conclusion, because if both personalities and vital skills are subject to change, then neither applicants' personalities nor their skills provide a good basis for choosing someone for a job.

(c) counts against the conclusion, because it suggests that personality differences between candidates are not very important (since everyone can develop a good personality), and also that for some jobs, those which involve skills which not everyone can acquire, differences between candidates in terms of their skills are very important.

3   The answer is (a).

(a) supports the conclusion by mentioning a disastrous possible conse-quence for light-skinned people of exposure to the sun – the likelihood of getting skin cancer.

(b) is not relevant to the conclusion, since it mentions the effect of exposure to the sun only for dark-skinned people, and the conclusion concerns only the effect for light-skinned people.

(c) does not support the conclusion. It mentions a way in which light-skinned people can avoid some exposure to the sun – by using sun creams. But it does not say anything about why they should avoid exposure.

4   The answer is (a).

(a) supports the conclusion by pointing out an *economic* benefit of installing insulation – reducing fuel costs. So even if it is expensive to install insulation, in the long run you may save money by doing so.

(b) does not support the conclusion, since it does not mention an *economic* benefit of installing insulation. It simply refers to the benefit in terms of comfort.

(c) does not support the conclusion, because it mentions a disadvan-tage of some types of insulation – that they can cause damp. This gives no reason to think that installing insulation is economical. In fact it suggests that it may lead to extra costs, for treatment of damp.

5   The answer is (c).

(c) supports the conclusion by showing that imprisonment of young offenders leads to an increase in crime, since it makes them more likely to re-offend.

(a) does not support the conclusion that young offenders should not be imprisoned. It simply suggests a way of using their time in prison construc-tively – to teach them job skills.

(b) does not support the conclusion, because it focuses only on over-crowding in prisons and the expense of building new ones, whereas the conclusion focuses on the reduction of crime as a reason for not using impris-onment for young offenders.

6   The answer is (c).

(c) supports the conclusion by showing that it was physically impossible for Sam to have committed the murder.

(a) does not support the conclusion, because even if Sally both wanted to commit the murder and could have done it, this does not show that Sam could not have done it.

(b) does not support the conclusion, since Sam could have committed the murder even if he had nothing to gain by doing so.

7   The answer is (b).

(b) supports the conclusion by showing that those who have a vegetarian diet avoid eating something which can be bad for health – the animal fats which can cause heart disease.

(a) does not support the conclusion, because it mentions only a deficiency of vegetarians diets – the lack of certain vitamins – which might suggest that a vegetarian diet could be bad for health.

(c) does not support the conclusion because it mentions something which is beneficial to health, but which is absent from vegetarian diets.

8   The answer is (b).

(b) supports the conclusion by showing that something undesirable would happen if many parents did not have their children vaccinated against polio – that there would be outbreaks of the disease every few years.

(a) does not support the conclusion, because it simply tells us what some parents think about the risk of side effects from the vaccine. This gives us no information about the benefits of vaccination.

(c) on its own does not support the conclusion. It might suggest that there is little need to have children vaccinated against polio, since the risk of becoming infected is very low. However, the reason why the risk is low may be because there has been a high level of vaccination amongst the population. If this information were added to (c), (c) could function as part of the reasoning to support the conclusion.

9   The answer is (a).

(a) supports the conclusion because if non-swimmers avoid activities in which there is a high risk of drowning, and swimmers engage in these activities, then this could explain why amongst those who drown there are more swimmers than non-swimmers.

(b) does not support the conclusion, because it does not say whether most of those who fail to wear life jackets are swimmers.

(c) does not support the conclusion, because it says nothing about non-swimmers. It explains why even those who can swim may drown, but this gives us no reason to think that amongst those who drown there will be more swimmers than non-swimmers.

10 The answer is (c).

(c) supports the conclusion by showing that some chewing gums cause tooth decay.

(a) does not support the conclusion, because it simply tells us about the chewing gums which can be good for the teeth.

(b) does not support the conclusion, because it suggests chewing any type of gum can have some good effect on the teeth.

Exercise 4: Identifying parts of an argument

In these answers, the reasons are numbered, 'Reason 1, Reason 2' etc. It does not matter which number you give to which reason, so don't worry if you have numbered them differently. What matters is the relationship between reasons and intermediate conclusions, and between reasons and main conclusions.

1 There is only one reason and a conclusion in this argument.

> *Reason*: You have to pay to go to the theatre or to listen to a concert.

> *Conclusion*: There's no good reason to object to paying for admission to museums and art galleries.

The argument takes for granted that there would be good reason to object to paying for admission to museums and art galleries only if admission to other cultural experiences were free.

2 The main conclusion is the last sentence, indicated by the word 'thus'. The rest of the passage describes a study which is assumed to provide evidence for this conclusion. We can regard the argument as having the following structure:

> *Reason 1*: A study by psychiatrists at the Royal Free Hospital in London compared treatments for two groups of about seventy patients suffering from depression.

and

Reason 2: In one group, patients were given twelve sessions of psychotherapy; in the other, they were given routine care from their general practitioner.

and

Reason 3: They all improved significantly over the next nine months.

and

Reason 4: there were no differences between the two groups in the rate and extent of improvement.

These four reasons taken together are intended to support:

Conclusion: Psychotherapy is thus no more effective than chatting with your GP.

3   The main conclusion is the last sentence, signalled by the phrase 'That is why'. Notice the word 'because' in the second sentence, indicating a reason. The argument has the following structure:

Reason 1: Passive smoking causes cancer.

This is offered in support of:

Intermediate conclusion: Smokers are putting our health at risk.

This intermediate conclusion, taken together with:

Reason 2: The one-third of people who smoke in public places are subjecting the rest of us to discomfort.

is offered in support of:

Main conclusion: That is why it is time to ban smoking in public places.

The intermediate conclusion and Reason 2 *could* be regarded as supporting the main conclusion independently, but the argument is stronger if they are taken as joint reasons for the conclusion.

4   There are two 'reason indicators' in this passage – 'because' in the first sentence, and 'the evidence for this is' in the second sentence. The main conclusion is the first part of the first sentence, and the argument can be set out as follows:

> *Reason 1*: Some drugs which appeared safe in animal tests have been harmful to humans.

and

> *Reason 2*: Aspirin and penicillin are poisonous to cats.

are intended, jointly, to support:

> *Intermediate conclusion*: Animals are too different from humans.

offered in support of:

> *Main conclusion*: Testing drugs on animals cannot give us the information we need in order to assess safety for humans.

5   The phrase 'this means that' suggests that a conclusion is being drawn in the second sentence, but the passage then goes on to draw a further conclusion in the last sentence. The structure is:

> *Reason*: The birth rate in European countries is declining very fast.

offered in support of:

> *Intermediate conclusion 1*: Even though people are living longer, eventually the size of the population will fall.

and

> *Intermediate conclusion 2*: there will be fewer and fewer people of working age to sustain an ageing population.

These two intermediate conclusions, taken together, support:

> *Main conclusion*: Either it will be necessary to raise the retirement age, or younger people will have to increase their productivity at work.

You may have been tempted to split the last sentence into two separate statements, and say that the argument has two distinct main conclusions. It would be possible for an argument to have two main conclusions, if the reasoning supported two important but unrelated points. But in this passage the two points *are* related, in that if the retirement age were raised, it may not be necessary for younger people to increase their productivity, and vice versa. The argument is not claiming that it will be necessary to raise the retirement age *and* it will be necessary for younger people to increase their productivity at work. It is saying that *either* one *or* the other will be necessary.

6   This argument has a complicated structure, but it is not difficult to identify the conclusion, which is clearly indicated by the word 'so' in the last sentence. There are two reason indicators – 'because' and 'since' in the third sentence, and the phrase 'the result would be' in the second sentence indicates that a conclusion is being drawn there. The argument fits together as follows:

> *Reason 1*: [If tests on drivers for drugs such as cannabis are introduced], a zero limit may be set.

offered in support of:

> *Intermediate conclusion 1*: Someone with even a small amount of cannabis in the bloodstream could be prosecuted.

This intermediate conclusion, taken together with:

> *Reason 2*: Cannabis can remain in the bloodstream for up to four months.

is intended to support:

> *Intermediate conclusion 2*: Some people whose driving was not impaired could be prosecuted.

This intermediate conclusion then supports:

> *Intermediate conclusion 3*: This would be unfair.

which supports:

Main conclusion: So if drug tests are introduced, the limit should not be set at zero.

Notice that the conclusion is a hypothetical statement. Do you think that the argument is assuming something which isn't actually stated?

7   There are no argument indicators in this passage, so we have to ask what it is trying to get us to accept. It is trying to convince us that the cause of global warming may be something other than the burning of fossil fuels. The argument has the following structure:

Reason 1: It is clear that global warming is occurring.

and

Reason 2: The earth has experienced warmer climates and higher levels of carbon dioxide in previous ages, long before the current high level of fuel use.

are intended, jointly, to support:

Conclusion: We cannot be confident that [global warming] is caused by the burning of fossil fuels which produce high levels of carbon dioxide.

8   This argument has the same structure as the previous one:

Reason 1: If no one smoked, the revenue from taxes would be massively reduced.

and

Reason 2: Many smokers will die before collecting their full share of health and retirement benefits.

are offered jointly in support of:

Conclusion: Smoking related illnesses don't really cost the state as much as is often claimed.

9   There are a number of words here which can sometimes indicate that a conclusion is being presented – 'should' in the first and third sentences, 'cannot' in the second sentence, and 'must' in the last sentence. But they are

not much help to us, because it isn't possible for all four sentences to be the main conclusion. so we have to consider what it is trying to get us to accept. It gives four reasons for accepting the recommendation made in the first sentence, as follows:

> *Reason 1*: These transplants are expensive to perform.

and

> *Reason 2*: The risk of animal diseases being transmitted to humans cannot be ruled out.

and

> *Reason 3*: It should be possible to solve the shortfall of organs available for transplant by persuading more people to carry organ donor cards.

and

> *Reason 4*: A human organ must give a human being a better chance of survival.

are offered jointly to support

> *Conclusion*: Transplanting animal organs into humans should not be allowed.

10   The main conclusion appears in the final sentence, introduced by the words 'I conclude that'. Here is one way in which the structure of this argument can be set out.

> *Reason 1*: [If killing an animal infringes its rights, then] never may we destroy, for our convenience, some of a litter of puppies, or open a score of oysters when nineteen would have sufficed, or light a candle in a summer evening for mere pleasure, lest some hapless moth should rush to an untimely end.

> *Reason 2*: Nay, we must not even take a walk, with the certainty of crushing many an insect in our path, unless for really important business!

> *Reason 3*: Surely all this is childish.

These three reasons can be regarded as being intended, jointly, to support:

> *Intermediate conclusion*: It is absolutely hopeless to draw a line anywhere.

This intermediate conclusion is intended to support:

> *Main conclusion*: I conclude that man has an absolute right to inflict death on animals, without assigning any reason, provided that it be a painless death, but that any infliction of pain needs its special justification.

Exercise 7: Identifying assumptions in arguments

1   This passage concludes that there must be some innate differences between males and females in 'target-directed motor skills', on the grounds that even at the age of three, boys perform better than girls at these skills. The passage is clearly rejecting the other possible explanation which it mentions – that 'upbringing gives boys more opportunities to practise these skills'. The conclusion thus relies on the assumption that by the age of three boys cannot have had sufficient practice at these skills to account for their better performance.
   The assumption can be stated as follows:

> Before the age of three, boys cannot have had sufficient practice at target-directed motor skills to account for the fact that they perform better at these skills than girls of the same age.

The assumption functions as an additional reason.

2   This passage concludes that allowing parents to choose the sex of their children could have serious social costs. The two reasons given for this are that it would result in more males who could not find female partners, and it would lead to an increase in violent crime (since most violent crimes are committed by males). However, these two results would occur only if there was an increase in the male to female ratio in the population. So these two reasons rely on the assumption that if parents were allowed to choose the sex of their children, there would be a greater tendency to choose male offspring than to choose female offspring.
   The assumption can be stated as follows:

> If parents were able to choose the sex of their children, there would be more parents who chose to have boys than parents who chose to have girls.

This is an assumption which underlies the two basic reasons in the argument.

3   This argument concludes that the continued fall in house prices may have a beneficial effect. The reason given for this is that the middle classes will become enthusiastic campaigners for improvements in their environment. This reason is itself an intermediate conclusion, supported by the claim that when people live in a house for a long period of time, they develop a strong commitment to the local neighbourhood. This reason would not fully support the intermediate conclusion, without the assumption that if house prices continue to fall, the middle classes are likely to move house less frequently.

The assumption can be stated as follows:

> The continued fall in house prices is likely to lead to the typical middle class home owner occupying a house for a long period of time.

The assumption functions as an additional reason.

4   There are a number of unstated moves in this argument. The following outline of the structure of the argument identifies them.

> *Assumption 1*: The alarm did not wake me.
> *Reason 1*: The alarm easily wakes me if it goes off.

These two are taken together to support an unstated:

> *Intermediate conclusion 1 (Assumption 2)*: The alarm did not go off.

This in turn supports:

> *Intermediate conclusion 2*: If the money has been stolen, someone must have disabled the alarm system.

This, taken together with another unstated assumption:

> *Assumption 3*: Only a member of the security firm which installed the alarm could have disabled it.

supports the:

> *Main conclusion*: So the culprit must have been a member of the security firm which installed the alarm.

Assumptions 1 and 3 function as additional reasons. Assumption 2 functions as an intermediate conclusion.

5 The conclusion of this argument is that the few people who get measles are in greater danger than they would have been when measles was more common. Two reasons are offered as jointly supporting this claim – that many doctors have never seen a case of measles, and that the disease is difficult to diagnose without previous experience. It would not follow that measles sufferers were in *greater* danger in these circumstances if there were no effective treatments for measles.

The assumption can be stated as follows:

> The complications caused by measles can be treated (with some success) if measles is diagnosed.

The assumption functions as an additional reason.

6 The argument concludes that it is carbon monoxide, rather than nicotine, which causes the higher incidence of atherosclerotic disease amongst smokers than amongst non-smokers. The evidence it gives for this is that animals exposed to carbon monoxide for several months have shown symptoms of the disease. Two assumptions are needed in order for this evidence to support the conclusion – that smoking exposes one to carbon monoxide, and that carbon monoxide affects humans and animals in the same way.

The assumptions can be stated as follows:

> (a) Smokers experience higher exposure to carbon monoxide than do non-smokers.
> (b) Exposure to carbon monoxide has the same effect on humans as it does on animals.
> Both (a) and (b) function as additional reasons.

7 The conclusion of this argument is that reports of 'near-death' experiences are evidence that there is life after death. The reason given for this is that most of the patients who have reported experiences of this nature were neither drugged nor suffering from brain disease. This reason is offered as a rejection of the explanation by sceptics that the experiences are caused by changes in the brain which precede death, and which are similar to changes produced by drugs or brain disease. The argument relies on the assumption that these changes could occur only as a result of drugs or brain disease (which, of course, the sceptics would deny).

The assumption can be stated as follows:

The changes in the brain which produce altered states of consciousness could not occur in the absence of drugs or brain disease.

The assumption functions as an additional reason.

8   The argument concludes that the farm population in the USA has lost political power. The reason for this is that the growth of the urban population has increased the demand for food, resulting in the introduction of labour-saving technology on farms, and thus a reduction of numbers of workers engaged in farm labour and an accompanying further increase of people living and working in cities. Such changes would result in a loss of political power for the farm population only if such power depended upon the relative size of the farm population, so this must be assumed by the argument.

The assumption can be stated as follows:

The political power of the farm population is dependent upon its size relative to the rest of the population.

The assumption functions as an additional reason.

9   This argument concludes that it is important for the future of medicine to preserve wild plant species. It uses evidence from the past in order to draw this conclusion – that the progress of medicine over the past fifty years has depended upon the discovery of wonder drugs derived from wild plants. In order to draw the conclusion, it must be assumed that there are more discoveries of this kind yet to be made.

The assumption can be stated as follows:

The development of wonder drugs from wild plants is very likely to continue in the future.

Perhaps the most natural way to fit this assumption into the argument is as an intermediate conclusion, supported by the evidence that wonder drugs have been developed from wild plants in the past.

10   This passage argues from two facts – that much larger numbers of British people are travelling abroad for holidays now than thirty years ago, and that foreign travel is expensive – to the conclusion that British people had on average less money to spend thirty years ago. This conclusion does not follow unless it is assumed that if they had not had less money to spend thirty years ago than they do now, they would have been travelling abroad in greater numbers then.

The assumption can be stated as follows:

> The expense of foreign travel was the reason why the number of British people who travelled abroad for holidays was much smaller thirty years ago than it is now.

The assumption functions as an additional reason.

Exercise 8: Re-working Exercise 5

You first looked at this passage in Exercise 5, where you were asked to identify its main conclusion, and to write down a list of assumptions which you thought it made. Since this was before you read the section on identifying assumptions, you may have included some things which are not implicit reasons or implicit intermediate conclusions. You may also have missed some things which are assumptions of this kind. By comparing your answers both to Exercise 5 and to Exercise 8 with the answer below, you will be able to see how much the section on identifying assumptions has helped you to understand the passage.

The first step is to identify the conclusion, which is to be found, conveniently, at the end of the passage, clearly signalled by the word 'So':

> So we must tell the snipers not to fire at Bill Clinton [because of his sex life].

Next we must look for the reasons. Each of the first three paragraphs presents a major reason, and these, taken together, are intended to support the conclusion. These reasons are quite difficult to identify, because they are wrapped up in an entertaining journalistic style. The best way to tackle this is to remember that the article is trying to convince us that there is no justification for criticising Bill Clinton because of his sex life, and then to ask yourself, 'What major point is each paragraph attempting to make?'

The first two paragraphs aim to show that the two justifications which are usually given for examining a politicians's sex life do not in fact justify criticising Bill Clinton. The first paragraph deals with the first justification, and aims to show that this supposed justification can never be a good reason for criticising a politician. The supposed justification is 'if a man would cheat on his wife, he would cheat on his country'. Two lines of reasoning are offered to support the idea that this is not true – first some examples of good husbands who were bad Presidents and second the claim that many very skilled politicians also have a high sex drive.

The second paragraph aims to show that the second justification for examining a politician's sex life does not hold good in the case of Bill Clinton. The supposed justification is that since leaders provide examples to the nation they are hypocritical if they 'slip from grace'. It is claimed that Bill Clinton cannot be criticised on these grounds because he has never claimed to lead an entirely decent life.

In the third paragraph, the argument tries to show that it is inconsistent to criticise Bill Clinton on the grounds of his sexual misdemeanours, whilst at the same time regarding former President John F. Kennedy, who behaved in the same way, as a great President of whom the country was robbed by his assassination.

Let's summarise what we have identified so far. The passage argues that we should not criticise Bill Clinton because of his sex life, on the grounds that:

(a) it is not true that someone who would cheat on his wife would be dishonest in his capacity as a politician;
(b) Bill Clinton does not set a bad example to the nation; and
(c) it is inconsistent to criticise Bill Clinton because of his sex life whilst at the same time admiring former President John F. Kennedy.

Let us look in more detail at how these three claims are supposed to be established. The reasoning behind (a) above is as follows:

Reason 1: Gerry Ford and Jimmy Carter were, by most accounts, strong husbands but weak Presidents.

Reason 2: Pat Nixon knew where Dick was every night. The problem was that the American people could not be sure where he was during the day.

These two pieces of evidence are intended to support an unstated:

Intermediate conclusion 1: Someone can be a good husband but a bad President.

There seems to be another strand of reasoning, leading from:

Reason 3: it is a sad but obvious fact that, to many of those men to whom he gave unusual political nous, God handed out too much testosterone as well.

This can be seen as meant to support an unstated:

Intermediate conclusion 2: We should expect some highly talented politicians to 'cheat on their wives'.

Intermediate conclusion 1 and Intermediate conclusion 2, taken together, are intended to support (a) above – also not explicitly stated:

Intermediate conclusion 3: It is not true that 'if a man would cheat on his wife, he would cheat on his country'.

The reasoning behind (b) above is as follows:

Reason 4: Bill Clinton, unlike many senior US politicians, has never publicly claimed that he has led an entirely decent life.

This is intended to support an unstated:

Intermediate conclusion 4: Bill Clinton is not hypocritical about sexual morality.

This, taken together with:

Reason 5: The second excuse for prurience towards rulers is that leaders, tacitly or explicitly, set examples to the nation and thus their own slips from grace are hypocritical.

is intended to support (b) – also unstated:

Intermediate conclusion 5: Bill Clinton does not set a bad example to the nation.

The final paragraph describes the way in which people honour the memory of JFK, and also alludes to the stories which circulate about his sex life, which were not given publicity during his lifetime. Two claims underlie this paragraph, but are not explicitly stated. They are:

Reason 6 (unstated): Former President John F. Kennedy is widely regarded as having been a potentially great President.

Reason 7 (unstated): John F. Kennedy was guilty of sexual misdemeanours.

These two, taken together, are intended to support (c), also unstated:

Intermediate conclusion 6: It is inconsistent to criticise Bill Clinton because of his sex life whilst at the same time admiring former President John F. Kennedy.

Now let's list the unstated assumptions which this analysis identifies:

1 Someone can be a good husband but a bad President.
2 We should expect some highly talented politicians to 'cheat on their wives'.
3 It is not true that 'if a man would cheat on his wife, he would cheat on his country'.
4 Bill Clinton is not hypocritical about sexual morality.
5 Bill Clinton does not set a bad example to the nation.
6 Former President John F. Kennedy is widely regarded as having been a potentially great President.
7 Former President John F. Kennedy was guilty of sexual misdemeanours.
8 It is inconsistent to condemn Bill Clinton for his sexual misdemeanours, whilst regarding John F. Kennedy as a potentially great President.

If you have identified some of these assumptions, you may find yourself questioning the truth of them, or wondering whether they do indeed support the main conclusion. If so, you are ready to move on to the next section – 'Evaluating reasoning'. You may wish to look at this passage again later, and attempt to evaluate it for yourself.

Exercise 9: Identifying flaws

1 This passage asserts that a fantastic basketball team could be created, and concludes from this that the game would thereby become exciting for fans everywhere. We may doubt whether it is true that a fantastic basketball team could be created if the best player from each of the best teams formed a new club. All these 'best players' may have identical rather than complementary skills. However, we are not concerned with evaluating the truth of reasons in this exercise, so we should ask 'If it is true that a fantastic basketball team could be created if the best player from each of the best teams formed a new club, does it follow that basketball would then become an exciting game for fans everywhere. No – the evidence that a basketball team composed of extremely talented players could be created is insufficient to show that this would produce an exciting game for spectators. Perhaps it would not be exciting to watch one super-team playing against weaker opposition, and perhaps the excitement of basketball for fans depends upon seeing one's home team as having a chance of winning.

2   This is an example of the flaw of assuming that because two things have occurred together, one has caused the other. The fact that crimes have been committed when the moon is full is not a good reason to believe that the full moon causes people to commit crimes.

3   This argument draws a conclusion about one individual from evidence about what is generally true of members of the group to which that individual belongs. If we took the first sentence to mean that *every* young person today has more formal education than their grandparents had, then the conclusion about Wilma would follow. But it is more reasonable to construe the first sentence as meaning that *in general* young people today have more formal education than their grandparents had. If that is the claim, then there may be exceptions and Wilma may be one of those exceptions. Perhaps her grandparents were unusual in their generation in having a university education, and perhaps Wilma dropped out of education at an early stage.

4   The conclusion is that neither marijuana nor LSD can be harmful. The reason given for this is that doctors use them as painkillers for cancer patients. The conclusion does not follow, since doctors may have to use drugs which are harmful when the alternative – leaving the patient to suffer severe pain – is worse.

5   This passage tells us that adolescents have a higher requirement for iron than that of the rest of the population. It concludes from this that the reason why adolescents often suffer from anaemia is not that they have insufficient iron in their diets. However, if their requirement for iron is greater than normal, it is much more reasonable to conclude that their anaemia *could* be caused by insufficient iron in their diets. There is a question about the meaning of 'insufficient' in the conclusion. Adolescents suffering from anaemia may have an amount of iron in their diets which would be sufficient for all other people. But if their requirement for iron is greater, then this amount will be insufficient for them.

6   This argument concludes that if people in the West switched to a Japanese diet, then instead of dying from heart attacks, they would die from the diseases which are the most common causes of death in Japan. It bases this conclusion on two claims – that diet is an important cause of disease, and that heart attacks in the West are caused by diet. However, the evidence is insufficient to establish the conclusion, since diet may be an important cause of disease without being the only cause of disease. Hence the diseases common in Japan may be caused not by diet, but by genetic factors, or by environmental conditions. The passage does not settle the question as to

what causes strokes and cancers of the stomach amongst the Japanese. So we cannot be confident that changing to a Japanese diet would increase the incidence of these diseases amongst Westerners.

7   This passage concludes that cooking must have been invented 400,000 years ago, based on the evidence that fires, which would have been necessary for cooking, were being used at that time. But the passage establishes only that fire was *necessary* in order for cooking to be invented, not that it was *sufficient*. Perhaps the first use of fire was for warmth or to deter predators, and maybe cooking was not invented until some time later. This is an example of a common flaw – that of treating a necessary condition as if it were a sufficient condition.

8   This passage argues from the unreliability of a witness to the conclusion that what the witness said must have been false. But the evidence is insufficient for us to draw this conclusion. The most we can conclude is that Fred may not have been in the vicinity of the shop when the fire was started. Without further evidence we cannot conclude that he must have been somewhere else.

9   The conclusion of this argument is that most people could be musical geniuses if they practised hard enough. The evidence offered for this is that a number of composers (presumably musical geniuses) wrote their masterpieces only after a long period of training in composition. Two questionable moves have to be made in order for this evidence to be taken to support the conclusion. First it must be assumed that the practice which these composers had was *necessary* in order for them to write masterpieces. Maybe this is not too wild an assumption, but it is just possible that it was not practice, but maturity, which was required in order for them to write masterpieces. The more serious flaw is to conclude that because some people could write masterpieces as a result of practising hard, anyone could do so if they practised hard. This is to treat the necessary condition of practising or training in composition (if we concede that it *is* a necessary condition) as a sufficient condition for composing masterpieces. Perhaps what is also needed is a certain talent which not everyone possesses.

10   This argument concludes that there cannot be any link between being poor and committing crimes. The evidence it produces for this is that many poor people never commit a crime. But this evidence is insufficient to establish the conclusion. Even if many poor people never commit a crime, it may be true that some poor people who do commit crimes would not have done so if they had not been poor. So there could be a link between poverty and crime such that poverty makes *some* people more likely to commit crimes.

Exercise 10: Evaluating further evidence

1   The answer is (e).

(e) weakens the conclusion by giving an alternative explanation as to why those children who participate in school sports activities are less likely to fight. This alternative explanation is that those with a tendency to fight are not allowed to participate in school sports activities.

(a) has no impact on the conclusion. The supervision by adults of sports activities at school may explain why there was little fighting during sports. But the conclusion is about why those who participate in sports are less likely to fight at any time during school hours, and not just during sports activities.

(b) does not weaken the conclusion, since even if the participants in school sports activities are discouraged from being extremely aggressive, the physical activity of sport may be such as to channel aggressive energy into non-aggressive competition.

(c) at first sight looks as if it is contradicting the statement that children who do not participate in sports fight more than those who do. So you may have been tempted to pick (c). But 'tend to be more aggressive physically' does not mean 'tend to fight more'. It means 'have a greater underlying tendency towards aggression'. If this were true, and it were also true that these children fight less, this would strengthen the conclusion that participation in sport is channelling physical aggression which might otherwise be released through fighting.

(d) is irrelevant to the conclusion. The time during the school day at which fights usually occur makes no difference to the explanation as to why those who do not participate in school sports activities are more likely to fight.

2 The answer is (d).

(d) weakens the argument by showing that if businesses did what is recommended – i.e. reduced salaries for employees without advanced engineering degrees – this could eventually be to the disadvantage of engineering businesses. Although it may have the desirable effect of persuading more engineering graduates to take PhDs (and thereby increase the numbers of engineering teachers), it might also result in fewer enrolments of students on undergraduate engineering courses. In the long term this could lead to a shortage of good applicants for jobs in engineering, which would be against the interests of businesses.

(a) is irrelevant to the conclusion. If 'the sciences' do not include engineering, then (a) is not even on the same topic as the argument. If 'the sciences' do include engineering, then (a) adds nothing to the information in the passage that enrolment in engineering courses has increased.

(b) does not weaken the argument. It simply emphasises the problem – the need to attract more engineers into teaching – to which the argument offers a solution.

(c) has no impact on the argument. The high salaries paid by businesses to those with advanced engineering degrees are likely to tempt these people away from teaching. This makes no difference to the recommendation to solve the problem of the shortage of engineering teachers by reducing salaries for those without advanced degrees.

(e) has no impact on the argument. The argument is about a way of increasing the incentive for engineering graduates to pursue post graduate studies. The funding of research programmes would not increase this incentive, unless it made generous awards to potential students. (e) makes no claim that businesses fund generous awards to students.

3   The answer is (e).

(e) strengthens Joan's claim by providing evidence that some heroin addicts are likely to commit serious crimes in order to get supplies of the drug. This supports the claim that the amount of serious crime may be reduced if heroin addicts were given free supplies of the drug.

(a) does not strengthen Joan's claim, it weakens it. If heroin addicts were more likely to be violent when under the influence of heroin, they might commit crimes at such times. Providing them with free heroin would not reduce the amount of crime, if any, committed by heroin addicts.

(b) does not strengthen Joan's claim, because she is not trying to show that supplying heroin to addicts would make economic sense. She is claiming simply that it would reduce crime.

(c) does not strengthen Joan's claim, for the same reason that (b) does not strengthen it.

(d) does not strengthen Joan's claim because it concerns crime which is not related to the use of heroin. This tells us nothing about the effectiveness of Joan's proposed method of reducing drug-related crime.

4   The answer is (a).

If (a) is true, then there is a good reason for the automobile association to continue testing direction indicators, since if they do not, the numbers of defective direction indicators may increase. Hence (a) weakens the case for stopping inspection of direction indicators.

(b) on its own does not weaken the argument. It seems to offer a reason for making sure that direction indicators are in good working order. But this does not weaken the recommendation to stop inspecting them, unless (as (a) suggests) stopping the inspections would result in more faulty indicators.

(c) does not weaken the recommendation, unless there is reason to believe that the inspection procedures need to be as thorough as those in neighbouring states. (c) does not provide such a reason.

(d) does not weaken the recommendation to stop testing direction indicators. It appears to be offering a reason in support of the recommendation, but in fact it makes no difference either way. Even if automobiles fail the inspection on the grounds of other safety defects, there may still be automobiles with defective indicators on the roads.

(e) does not weaken the argument, although it may look as if it is offering a reason for retaining inspection of indicators. Inspecting them would not bring to light other defects not covered by the safety inspection system. So (e) is irrelevant to the question as to whether direction indicators should be inspected.

5   The answer is (d).

The researchers concluded that if parents monitored (presumably meaning 'controlled') the amount of time which their children spent watching television, the children's performance in school would benefit. So the researchers were assuming that the relationship they found between the hours the children spent watching television and their level of performance in school was evidence that watching for longer periods *caused* poorer performance. The researchers had discovered a correlation, but a correlation between two things does not necessarily mean that one thing causes the other. (See the discussion on p. 53.) (d) strengthens the idea that there is a causal connection. If differences in performance are less when hours watching television are roughly the same for all children, then it is likely that differences in time spent watching television causes differences in performance.

(a) gives more detail about the figures upon which the claim in the first sentence is based, so it strengthens the statement that if children watched between two and three hours of television per day, they were likely to perform less well in school. This is stronger evidence that there is a correlation, but gives no extra evidence of a causal connection. So it does not strengthen the conclusion, which relies on the assumption that there is a causal connection. Provided we assume that there is a causal connection between amount of television viewing and school performance, (b) could be regarded as giving an additional reason why school performance might improve if parents monitored their children's television viewing. But since (b) does nothing to strengthen the idea that there is a causal connection, it does not strengthen the conclusion of the researchers.

(c) does not strengthen the idea that watching television for two or more hours per day causes poorer performance in school. Instead it introduces a new factor – the amount of time spent reading – which may have an effect on school performance.

(e) does not strengthen the idea of a causal connection, because although it suggests that some children replaced their television watching with reading, it does not comment upon how this affected their performance in school.

6 The answer is (a).

(a) weakens the argument by showing that even if ex-prisoners do not pursue the occupation for which they have prepared whilst in prison, the skills they have learnt during training in prison may nevertheless be of use in whatever occupation they take up.

(b) provides an *objection* to scrapping career training programmes in prison. But this is not the same as weakening the argument, because it has no impact on the claim that it is *unwise* to continue such programmes since they do not achieve their aims.

(c) mentions an advantage of prison career training programmes, thereby to some extent weakening the claim that it is unwise to continue them. But this does not weaken the argument as much as (a), which shows that the claim upon which the conclusion of the argument is based – that the programmes do not achieve their aim (which we can assume is to provide skills which will be useful in future employment) – is not true.

(d) does not weaken the argument, because it simply emphasises that training programmes have the goal which the argument claims they do not achieve. (d) tells us nothing about whether they achieve that goal, hence has no impact on the conclusion that these programmes should be scrapped.

(e) does not weaken the argument, because the argument relies on the claim that prisoners choose not to pursue the occupation for which they have trained whilst in prison. This does not imply that they have no choice whilst in prison, nor does (e) imply that they will not change their choice of occupation after leaving prison.

7 The answer is (e).

(e) weakens the argument by providing evidence that the physiological changes recorded by a lie detector may result from stress other than the stress caused by lying. This suggests that, contrary to what the conclusion claims, reliable lie detection is not possible.

(a) has no impact on the argument, because reliable lie detection may be possible, even if the machines are expensive and require careful maintenance.

(b) suggests that for some people who are lying, lie detectors will indicate symptoms of only moderate stress. But this does not weaken the claim that reliable lie detection is possible.

(c) does not weaken the argument, because it does not suggest that it is impossible to find and train the personnel who can use lie detection instruments effectively.

(d) does not weaken the argument, because reliable lie detection may be possible even if some people misuse or abuse lie detecting equipment.

Exercise 11: Offering alternative explanations

These answers identify the fact and the explanation offered in each passage. They then give one or more possible alternative explanations. You may be able to think of other possible explanations.

1 *Fact*: Public confidence in the police force is declining at the same time as fear of crime is growing.
   Explanation: Fear of crime is caused by lack of confidence in the police.
   Alternative explanation: Fear of crime is caused by people's belief that the incidence of crime is increasing.

2 *Fact*: The divorce rate has increased greatly over the last thirty years.
   Explanation: There are more unhappy marriages than there used to be.
   Alternative explanation: It is now easier to obtain a divorce, and the stigma associated with divorce has gone. (Hence there may have been just the same percentage of unhappy marriages in the past, but people did not divorce because it was difficult or because others would disapprove.)

3 *Fact*: The human race has never received a well-authenticated communication from beings elsewhere in the universe.
   Explanation: The only intelligent life in the universe is on our planet.
   Alternative explanations: There is intelligent life elsewhere in the universe and

   • they don't want to communicate with us; or
   • they don't know we are here; or
   • we have failed to recognise their communications.

4 *Fact*: Whenever a new road is built, the density of traffic in that area increases.
   Explanation: The number of cars per head of population is increasing.
   Alternative explanation: When new roads are built, the average number

of journeys per motorist increases (i.e. when roads are better, people have more incentive to drive).

5 *Fact*: The number of people taking holidays in British resorts declined last summer.
Explanation: The weather was bad in Britain last summer.
Alternative explanations:

- For financial reasons fewer people took holidays.
- Prices for holidays abroad were reduced.
- There was bad publicity about pollution on British beaches.

Exercise 12: Identifying and evaluating explanations

Each of these answers identifies the fact or facts for which explanations are offered, identifies the possible explanations offered in the text, and suggests some other possible explanations. You may have thought up different possible explanations. We leave you to draw your own conclusions as to which explanation is the most plausible, or to think about evidence which could be sought to in order to settle this question.

1 (a) *Fact*: Girls perform better than boys in GCSE exams.
   (b) *Explanations in text*:
       - Girls have clearer goals and are more focused – boys have no idea what they want to do after GCSE.
       - Boys do not want to appear swotty – study is not seen as bad for girls' image.
       - Boys get less attention from teachers than girls do.
   (c) *Other possible explanations* (some suggested by comments in text):
       - Teachers' lower expectations of boys' abilities cause boys to perform less well than they could.
       - Boys are unable to concentrate or organise themselves, and lack motivation.
       - Girls are cleverer than boys.
       - Girls work harder than boys.
       - Girls reach intellectual maturity earlier than boys.

2 In this example there are a number of facts for which explanations are offered.
   (a) *Fact*: Fewer people were killed on Britain's roads last year than in any year since 1926.

(b) *Explanations in text*:
- There is better paramedic treatment at the roadside and better medical care.
- The figures are misleading because deaths which occur as a result of road accidents are counted as road deaths only if the death occurs within 30 days of the accident, and now people are kept alive longer by modern medical techniques.
- There has been a decline in the numbers of vulnerable road users such as pedestrians and cyclists.

(c) *Other possible explanations*:
- Roads are safer, due to better road construction, and/or safer driving.
- Cars are safer for their occupants, due to seat-belts, air-bags, crumple zones, side-impact bars, better brakes and so on.

(a) *Fact*: Child casualties are proportionally higher in Britain than in other European countries.

(b) *Explanation in text*: Children in Britain have to walk home from school in the dark in winter.

(c) *Other possible explanation*: There are more child pedestrians in areas of heavy traffic in Britain than in other European countries.

(a) *Fact*: The number of children killed on the roads and the number of serious injuries on the roads have both increased.

(b) *Explanations in text*:
- Roads are more dangerous.
- Drivers make mistakes because they feel too insulated in modern cars.

(c) *Other possible explanation*: There is more traffic on the roads.

3 (a) *Fact*: A statue of the Virgin Mary has been observed to appear to shed tears.

(b) *Explanation in text*: It is likely that the statue is made of permeable material with an impermeable glaze, and that it has a hollow centre. If the glaze over the eyes is scratched, droplets of water appear, and it looks as if the statue is weeping.

(c) *Other possible explanation*: The statue is weeping, and this is a miracle.

With this example you may find it impossible to think up any further possible explanations, but you should have a lively discussion as to which of these is more plausible, and how you might find out.

Exercise 13: Practising the skills

1 Television – a force for good in our nation's prisons

1 *Conclusion*: This passage makes clear at the outset the position for which it is arguing. The conclusion, which appears in the first paragraph, is that it is right to proceed with the proposal to allow the prison population to watch television.

2 *Reasons/assumptions*: The question 'Why?' at the beginning of the second paragraph tells us that reasons are about to be offered, and they are further signalled by the word 'First' which immediately follows, and the phrase 'The second reason', at the beginning of the third paragraph. However, in the second paragraph, it appears that there is not just one reason, but a number of reasons grouped together, one of them signalled by the word 'Furthermore'.

The following reasons can be identified:

1 Watching television is a better way for prisoners to spend their time.
2 Watching television makes prisoners easier to guard.
3 Prisoners who watch television are more likely to end up like the rest of us.
4 Paying for the privilege of watching television increases responsibility.
5 Paying for the privilege of watching television makes prisoners better fitted for 'earning and paying' once they leave prison.

Support for Reason 1 takes the form of a description of the ways in which prisoners may spend their time in the absence of television. Support is offered for Reason 3 by the observation that to deny television to prisoners cuts them off from social trends, thinking, entertainment and news which shape other citizens.

Some assumptions associated with these reasons are that television in prison can counteract the prison culture (the 'crime-behind-bars'); that one important purpose of imprisonment is rehabilitation; and – possibly – that if prisoners become more like the rest of us, they will be less likely to re-offend.

3 *Assessing truth of reasons/assumptions*: The truth of Reason 1 is hard to assess. Does it mean that if prisoners watch television, this is better for prisoners, and for prison officers, and for society? It probably does mean it's better for prisoners, given the word 'humane' in the last sentence, and perhaps it is true that television would be more enjoyable for some prisoners

than some of the alternatives mentioned – but the author may be implying not simply that it would be more enjoyable, but that it would be more worthy, and better for the character of prisoners. If it also means it would be better for prison officers, this ties up with Reason 2, and seems like a reasonable claim. The author does seem to think it would be better for society, in view of the emphasis on returning prisoners to ordinary life.

The truth of Reason 3 can be questioned. Watching television will give prisoners access to the same information as that available to other citizens, but it doesn't follow that it will lead them to hold the same social values. The values of the 'prison culture' – if there is such a thing – may dominate; also it is possible, though perhaps not very likely, that the reminder from television programmes that others are leading more pleasant lives may lead to alienation and resentment, rather than identification.

Reason 4 is probably true of many prisoners, in that they are likely to want the privilege of watching television, and that making this conditional upon earning and paying could give them a feeling of control over this aspect of their life.

Nevertheless, reason 5 is questionable. Whether or not the habit of 'earning and paying' in prison will transfer to life outside prison will depend on additional factors – for example, the availability of work, the possession of skills, and so on.

The assumption that imprisonment should be for rehabilitation as well as punishment is generally accepted within the criminal justice system, though it may not be shared by some of the public. It is, however, reasonable, given that it is not feasible (except at great expense) to keep all criminals in prison for life, and it is not wise to free prisoners who are not fit to return to ordinary life.

4 *Authorities cited*: No authorities are mentioned in the article.

5 *Further evidence*: You may have commented here that there may be other countries where prisoners are allowed to watch television, and which may provide some evidence of the effects of this policy on security and rehabilitation.

6 *Explanations*: There are no explanations in the passage.

7 *Support for conclusion*: The conclusion claims that the policy is right 'pragmatically and in principle', but most of the reasoning concentrates on the pragmatic (i.e. practical) aspects – making prisoners easier to guard and better fitted for life outside prison. These would be good reasons for acting on the policy, provided it had no adverse effects and that there were no better ways of achieving the aims.

It is difficult to think of adverse effects of the policy, though some may claim that prisoners simply do not deserve to have privileges such as access to television. (This touches upon the aspect of 'principle' in the passage – the reference to a 'humane' policy, and the assumption that rehabilitation is an important aim of prison policy.) Or it may be claimed that the policy makes prison life appear to be insufficiently harsh to deter potential criminals. We leave you to consider (and possibly debate) the truth of these claims.

What better ways could there be of making prisoners easier to guard, and better fitted for returning to life outside prison? More prison officers may have some impact on the problem of 'crime-behind-bars', but this would be a costly solution. More productive work for prisoners and more education in prison may help rehabilitation, but there would still be some periods when prisoners were not engaged in work or education. Provision of television is relatively inexpensive, and probably worthwhile if it has the effects claimed in the passage.

2   The economic case for drugs

1   *Conclusion*: The whole of this passage presents reasons in favour of legalising drugs, and its conclusion is that 'drug legalisation would be a far superior policy to drug prohibition'.

2   *Reasons/assumptions*: The reasons are as follows:

1   Drug prohibition does not eliminate drug markets or drug use; it simply drives them underground.
    Support is offered for this in the claim that data in the US suggests that more than 30 per cent of the population aged 12 and over has used marijuana, and more than 10 per cent has used cocaine.
2   Drug prohibition increases violence.
    Two pieces of support are offered for this: that buyers and sellers of drugs cannot use the official justice system to resolve disputes; and the information given in the fifth paragraph about the homicide rate.
3   Prohibition plays a role in non-violent crime by diverting resources.
4   Prohibition facilitates corruption of the police, judges and politicians.
    The reasons given for this claim are that huge profits are at stake, and that legal channels of influence are not available.
5   Prohibition means diminished health.
    This claim is supported by the statements that quality and purity of drugs are uncertain in a black market, and that users are more likely to use unhealthy methods such as injection.

In addition, evidence is offered about a rise in deaths due to alcoholism during prohibition, which is attributed by the article to adulteration of alcohol.

6 Prohibition means drug suppliers and drug users gain at the expense of taxpayers in general.

This is supported by the observation that society cannot levy taxes on prohibited drugs, nor collect income tax from those working in the drug trade.

The argument assumes a causal connection between prohibition of alcohol and an increase in the murder rate; assumes that any adverse effects from the legalisation of drugs would not be sufficient to outweigh its advantages; and assumes that there are significant similarities between alcohol and drugs.

3 *Assessing truth of reasons/assumptions*: Reason 1 is true – there is sufficient evidence from convictions for possession and sale of drugs to show that prohibition does not eliminate drug use. The source of the figures for illegal drug use in the US is not mentioned, but even if these figures are not accurate, there is no reason to doubt that illegal drug use occurs.

The first comment offered in support of Reason 2 provides a plausible explanation as to why violence may occur during drug prohibition, but does not provide evidence of its occurrence. The evidence given in the fifth paragraph assumes that because there was a rise in the homicide rate after prohibition of alcohol and drugs was introduced, and a fall after alcohol prohibition was repealed, prohibition must have caused the rise in the homicide rate. This assumption is questionable, and the evidence does not allow us to distinguish between the effects of alcohol prohibition and those of drug prohibition. The dramatic fall in the murder rate after alcohol prohibition was repealed suggests a stronger connection with alcohol than with drug prohibition. The increase in the murder rate after the 1960s is attributed to an increase in drug law enforcement, with which it coincided. But the increase in law enforcement may have been a response to the increase in the murder rate, and was not necessarily a cause of it. More information would be needed in order to assess the plausibility of the assumption of a causal connection – for example, whether the victims and the murderers were known to be involved in drugs trading.

In relation to Reason 3, it is clearly true that police who are spending a great deal of time on drugs-related offences cannot spend that time on other forms of crime, although it is possible that resources for the police could be increased to enable them to deal with all crime.

Reason 4 is not supported by evidence of corruption, although it may be true that prohibition makes it easier to corrupt police, judges and politicians.

Reason 5 may well be true, since drug dealers aiming to maximise profit will not be too concerned about the quality and purity of their product. If drugs were legalised, there would be quality controls on the substances sold, and there could be more control over hygiene in injection of drugs.

Reason 6 is true – illegal employment and consumption are not taxed.

The argument doesn't mention any adverse effects of drug legalisation, but it must be assuming that any such effects are not sufficient to outweigh the benefits which it lists. It acknowledges that prohibition probably reduces demand by some customers, which implies that legalisation would probably increase demand. It may also increase the number of customers. This may have adverse effects on health, contrary to the claim in reason 5. One problem for reason 5 is that no distinction is made between drugs which in themselves are not very damaging to health, and those which are harmful and addictive. Legalisation of soft drugs may have the health benefits claimed, but legalisation of hard drugs may lead to an increase in the use of harmful and addictive substances.

4   *Authorities cited*: No authorities are mentioned in the article.

5   *Further evidence*: Evidence from countries where drug use is tolerated (e.g. the Netherlands) could be sought, and may give some indication as to the effects of decriminalisation on drug use and health of the population.

6   *Explanations*: The rise in the homicide rate in the USA is explained as due to the introduction of drug and alcohol prohibition laws (after 1910), and to an increase in drug law enforcement (late 1960s). The plausibility of this explanation, and the need to look at evidence in more detail has been commented on under *Assessing truth of reasons/assumptions* above.

The rise in deaths due to alcoholism relative to other proxies for alcohol consumption is tentatively explained as due to an increase in consumption of adulterated alcohol. Another possible explanation is that the level of consumption per consumer increases during prohibition. It would be difficult to establish which of these was true, and both suggest adverse effects of prohibition.

7   *Support for conclusion*: The principal problem for the argument is that the claim that drug legalisation would be *far superior* to prohibition requires consideration of possible adverse effects of prohibition and showing that these do not outweigh the benefits. But the argument does not consider any possible adverse effects. No distinction is made between drugs which are harmful to health and highly addictive (e.g. heroin), and drugs which may not be seriously damaging to health (e.g. cannabis). If all drugs were legalised,

there may be health benefits for soft drug users, as a result of greater control over the quality and purity of the drug; but if there were an increase in hard drug use (and the author concedes that although prohibition does not eliminate drug use, it may reduce demand) there may be a deterioration in health for some users.

There may also be adverse economic effects. The benefits of increased taxation and reduction in police costs may, if drug use increased, be outweighed by increased costs in terms of health care and working time lost.

The argument could perhaps have been strengthened by claiming that individuals should be allowed to choose whether to harm their own health by using drugs, particularly since they are allowed to do this with other drugs – alcohol and nicotine.

3   There are greater dangers to children than mobile phones

1   *Conclusion*: The conclusion indicator 'therefore', which occurs in the sixth paragraph indicates that the conclusion is that we should 'get the priorities in the right order' – that is, 'We should stop the parents using mobiles in the car, not the children using them in the street'.

2   *Reasons/assumptions*: The reasons can be summarised as follows:

1   Only three effects of mobiles have been proved.
Associated with this reason is the assumption that none of these three effects is sufficiently worrying for us to stop children using mobile phones.
The first of these effects is a slight heating of the brain, which is dismissed on the grounds that 'we might as well prevent children from wearing hats'. Hence it is assumed that using a mobile phone does not heat the brain any more than does wearing a hat.
The second effect is a speeding up of reaction times, which is worrying enough to 'warrant caution and further research'.
The third is 'an increased chance of death or injury from using a mobile whilst driving' – obviously irrelevant to whether children should use mobile phones, since they do not drive, but evidence for the first part of the conclusion – that we should stop parents using mobiles in the car.
2   There are serious threats to the health of children.
These are listed as teenage pregnancy, drugs and abduction. It is assumed that these are more serious threats to health than any effects of mobile phone use by children.

3 Children should be allowed to take responsibility for their own choices. This is not explicitly stated, but is alluded to in the seventh paragraph.

4 The use of mobile phones allows teenagers to have some independence.

There is an additional assumption – that we do not need to worry about any as yet undiscovered effects of mobile phone use.

You may have listed as a reason the comparison with what might have been said about watching television in the early days, and this comment is certainly trying to influence us in favour of thinking that it is ridiculous to be cautious about the use of mobile phones. In order to assess the contribution this makes to the reasoning, you need to consider ways in which watching television and using mobile phones might differ.

3 *Assessing truth of reasons/assumptions*: Without examining the source of the information about effects of mobile phone use, it is not possible to assess the truth of the claims. However, the truth of some of the assumptions is questionable. If there is a 'biological effect' – the speeding up of reaction times – which 'warrants caution and further research', why should we assume that this effect is not sufficiently worrying for us to stop children using mobile phones? Moreover, we cannot substantiate the assumption that other threats to the health of children are more serious, without knowing whether this speeding up of reaction times *is* an indication of a serious problem.

Reason 3 is true in relation to many choices which children may make, but there are some areas – use of drugs and alcohol, for example – where we think it right not to allow them a choice. If mobile phone use were shown to be seriously dangerous, it might be reasonable to include it in this category.

Reason 4 is true to the extent that a mobile phone provides one means of allowing teenagers to be independent 'while preserving an invisible electronic umbilical cord'.

4 *Authorities cited*: The article refers to a report by 'distinguished experts', but we are not told who these experts are. In principle, it would be possible to trace this report and ask the appropriate questions about the reliability of the authors.

5 *Further evidence*: You might have commented that further studies could be done (the author suggests this also), and that it would be wise not to let children use mobile phones until more is known. This would be to appeal to the 'precautionary principle', which is often mentioned in discussions about risks. In recent years it has been applied to risks of catching Creutzfeld–Jakob Disease (CJD) from eating beef infected with Bovine Spongiform

Encephalopathy (BSE), and to the risk of genetically modified crops adversely affecting the environment. Where the principle is used, it is reasonable to consider not simply the degree of risk of something bad happening (which cannot always be assessed), but also how bad the feared consequence would be, and how costly or inconvenient it would be to take avoiding action. In relation to BSE and CJD, for example, although it could not be known how great was the risk of contracting CJD from eating beef on the bone, the terrible nature of the potential consequences (perhaps many people dying from a ghastly brain disease) was seen to outweigh the costs of banning the sale of beef on the bone. To use the precautionary principle in relation to children's use of mobile phones would be to say that children should be prevented (or at least strongly discouraged) from using mobile phones because the effects which *might* occur – children developing brain tumours – would outweigh the advantage of the convenience of using mobile phones.

6 *Explanations*: There is an explanation as to why the increased risk of death or injury from using a mobile whilst driving is still significant when the phone is hands-free. This is said to be because 'the driver visualises the disembodied other party and cannot see the road or its obstacles'. It is difficult to assess whether this is the correct explanation, though it seems plausible, and would help to explain why talking to someone else who is in the car doesn't seem to increase the chance of an accident. In any case, the *explanation* of the increased risk of an accident is less crucial to the argument than whether the claim itself – that there *is* an increased risk of an accident when using a mobile phone whilst driving – is true.

7 *Support for conclusion*: The evidence about increased risk of car accidents, if it is accurate, is a good reason for concluding that parents (and everyone else) should be prevented from using mobile phones whilst driving. However, this contributes nothing to the question as to whether children should be prevented from using mobile phones. There is no reason to think in terms of 'priorities' in relation to these two issues. If it were a fact that children are less at risk of ill-health from using a mobile phone than of being killed or injured by adults driving without due care or attention, this would not show that children should not be prevented from using mobile phones. The crucial questions in relation to that part of the conclusion are: how dangerous is mobile phone use for children, and do the dangers outweigh the benefits?

We cannot judge the dangers from the evidence presented, but given that it is not crucial for children to be able to use mobile phones, a more reasonable conclusion might be that we should err on the side of caution, and at least try to stop children using mobile phones until more is known.

The benefit of mobile phone use mentioned in the article – that it enables teenagers to have some independence 'while preserving an invisible electronic umbilical cord', does not seem sufficient to outweigh the risk, given that teenagers have always managed to have some independence.

The claim about the existence of greater dangers is irrelevant, since, again, we do not have to think in terms of priorities. The weakness of support from Reason 3 (that children should be allowed to take responsibility for their own choices) has already been mentioned – that it is reasonable to prevent or discourage children from doing things which would seriously harm them.

Overall the article does not strongly support the conclusion that we should not stop children from using mobile phones. Of course, there is a light-hearted tone to the passage, and newspaper articles are meant to be entertaining, so you may think that we should not expect serious reasoning. But this is a serious subject, and its conclusion is important. In the first edition of this book there was an article in the topic of BSE which made light hearted comments about mad cows being in the news again. Subsequent events have shown the seriousness of the BSE epidemic. Examples like this should remind us to look at even 'jokey' reasoning with a discerning eye.

Exercise 14: Drawing conclusions

1 The temperature must have dropped to below freezing point overnight.
2 It is likely that Gitta has flu.
3 The daffodils will probably flower late this year.
4 Jane's car must have travelled faster than Jim's.
5 If Ms Brown killed the murder victim, she must have poisoned him.

Exercise 15: Assessing implications

1 (a) *Probably false*: The passage states that the incidence of skin cancer is higher amongst professionals than amongst manual workers, which suggests that there are some cases amongst manual workers.
   (b) *Insufficient information*: If 20 per cent of cases occur amongst those aged 20 to 39, and 80 per cent amongst over 40s (though it may be less than 80 per cent, because some cases may occur amongst under 20s), it looks more likely that the risk is greater for over 40s. But we do not have enough information to conclude that (b) is false, first because it makes a general claim, and we have figures only about the

incidence in Sweden, and second because we do not know about any differences in lifestyles of the two age groups in Sweden which may account for the greater percentage of cases amongst the over 40s.

(c) *False*: The increased incidence of skin cancer in Sweden could be caused by exposure to sunlight, since more people from Sweden may be taking holidays in sunny countries. Of course, it may be true that exposure to sunlight is not the only cause of skin cancer, but it is false that the figures from Sweden indicate this.

(d) *Insufficient information*: Although we are told that only 20 per cent of cases occur in the 20 to 39 age group, and that exposure to sunlight is a significant cause of skin cancer, we do not know whether the higher number of cases amongst over 40s is attributable to greater exposure to sunlight for this group, or to a greater tendency for older people to succumb to skin cancer, even given equal exposure to that of younger people.

(e) *True*: We can conclude that the increased incidence of skin cancer in Sweden *may* be due to an increase in numbers holidaying in sunny countries. In answering 'true' to (e), we are not concluding that this is the cause. (e) merely states tentatively that it may be.

2 (a) *Insufficient information*: We are told only about the sample of 600 drivers. Even if most of them had an inflated sense of their own safety as car drivers, this information cannot support the claim that most drivers have an inflated sense of their safety. The drivers in this sample may not have been representative of drivers in general. They may have been chosen because of their unusual attitudes.

(b) *Probably true*: If most of the group overestimate their driving skills, then some of the 50 per cent who said they would drive at over 80 mph on a motorway must also overestimate their driving skills. Assuming that 80 mph is too fast, and that the drivers do as they say, then these drivers tend to drive too fast on motorways. Since these assumptions are not unreasonable, it is probably true that some drivers who overestimate their skills tend to drive too fast.

(c) *Probably false*: We are told that those most likely to overestimate their driving skills are young men. Since young men are likely to have had only a few years' driving experience, it is probably false that those with only a few years' driving experience do not overestimate their driving skills.

(d) *True*: The study demonstrated that forcing drivers to imagine that they had caused a serious accident made some of them change their judgement about the speed at which they would be prepared to drive. Assuming that the effect on their attitudes is long-term, and that they act in accordance with this changed judgement, some of them will drive more responsibly, with respect to speed, in the future. So it is true that imagining the accident may make them drive more responsibly in the future.

(e) *Insufficient information*: We are told that the drivers were asked to *imagine* the lack of confidence they might experience if they caused a serious accident. But this does not imply that they actually lost confidence in their driving as a result.

3 (a) *Probably true*: Although the passage refers to a ewe forming a bond with 'its own lamb', this use of the singular noun does not suggest that a ewe can form a bond with only *one* of its own lambs. The statement that the ewe 'rejects all others' is best understood as meaning that she rejects all except her own lambs.

(b) *Insufficient information, or probably false?* Strictly speaking we do not have enough information in this passage to conclude either that a ewe will or that she will not reject her own lamb if she is introduced to another lamb. However, given a few assumptions, we can conclude that (b) is probably false. First, if the ewe really believes she has given birth to another lamb, then presumably she can form bonds with both her own and the orphaned lamb in the same way that she could (we have assumed above) form bonds with both her own twin lambs. Second, unless the farmers are using this technique only with ewes whose own lambs have died shortly after birth, there would be no point in using the technique at all if it resulted in an orphaned lamb being accepted by the foster mother, whilst her own lamb was rejected.

(c) *True*: We are told that lack of maternal contact can cause behaviour abnormalities.

(d) *False*: We are told that farmers do rear orphaned lambs themselves. Such lambs may have behaviour abnormalities, but can nevertheless grow to adulthood.

(e) *True*: There is an 80 per cent chance of a ewe accepting, and thus of forming a bond with, an orphaned lamb, if the farmer uses the technique of fooling the ewe into thinking she has given birth to another lamb.

4 (a) *Insufficient information*: The passage makes it clear that scab and blowfly attacks cause damage to sheepskins. This may be sufficient reason for farmers to want to use sheep dip. Without further information, we cannot tell whether these parasites cause distress to sheep.

(b) *False*: There is some evidence of a possible link in fifty-eight of the cases examined.

(c) *Insufficient information*: Three of the people whose symptoms may have been caused by using sheep dip were wearing protective clothing. If these three people's symptoms were definitely caused by using sheep dip, then we could conclude that the clothing does not prevent damage to health when using sheep dip, and thus that (c) is false. But we do not know whether their symptoms were definitely caused by the use of the sheep dip.

(d) *False*: We are told that it is not known what the effects of exposure to sheep dip are. Even though we must conclude that (d) is false, this is not the same as saying that there is no justification for banning the use of sheep dip. Some people might argue that if there is any potential risk to health, its use should be banned.

(e) *Probably true*: There is some evidence of a potential risk, and the Ministry of Agriculture is sufficiently concerned to ensure that sheep dips are handled only by those with a certificate of competence.

Exercise 16: Identifying parallel arguments

1 The answer is (d). They both have the following structure:
Because Xs usually have characteristic Y, and
because Z has characteristic Y, it follows that
Z is probably an X.

In the original argument,
X = heroin addict
Y = needle marks on their arms
Z = Robert

In (d),
X = students
Y = age of less than 25 years
Z = Harold

The structure of (a) is:
Because Xs usually have Y, and
because Z is an X,
Z probably has Y.

The structure of (b) is:
    Because patients with X usually have Y,
    X probably causes Y.

The structure of (c) is:
    Because Xs have Y, and
    because people with Y do Z,
    Xs probably do Z.

The structure of (e) is:
    Because Xs usually have characteristic Y,
    most Xs probably do Z.

2 The answer is (b). The last sentence and (b) both reason as follows:
    X did (does) not cause Y,
    Y caused (causes) X

In the original passage,
    X = high infant mortality
    Y = the indifference of parents towards their children

In (b),
    X = lack of qualified workers in the poor sectors of an economy
    Y = low wages

The structure of (a) is:
    It was not X which caused Y,
    it was Z which caused Y.

The structure of (c) is:
    X does not cause Y,
    Y happens whether X happens or not.

The structure of (d) is:
    Those who do X cause harm to X and to Y.

The structure of (e) is:
    It was not considered worthy for Xs to do Y,
    but many Xs did Y.

3 The answer is (a). (a) and the passage both have the following underlying structure:

In one case (or in some cases), the absence of X has not prevented the occurrence of disastrous result Y.

Therefore, X does not have the disastrous results which it is supposed to have.

In the original passage,
X = rapid population growth
Y = political and economic decline

In (a),
X = smoking cigarettes
Y = chronic respiratory illnesses

(b) starts with a statement which could be seen as similar in structure to the first statement of the original passage:

Using expensive paint (the absence of cheap paint) did not remove the need to apply two coats (did not prevent disastrous result of having to apply two coats).

But the conclusion of (b) makes no reference to cheap paint not having the disastrous results it is supposed to have.

(c) could also be seen as starting off in a similar way to the passage:

Using less energy (the absence of high energy consumption) will not prevent an increase in oil imports.

But there is no suggestion that using less energy has been claimed to have disastrous results.

Neither (d) nor (e) even begins with a similar structure to the original passage.
(d) begins with: X causes Y for some Z
(e) begins with: Some X are Y and Z

Exercise 17: Applying and evaluating principles

Here are some suggested applications of the principles. You may have thought of different applications, so don't regard these suggestions as the only 'right' answers.

1 People who never travel by public transport should not have to pay that portion of taxes which subsidise public transport.

2 We should not have laws which prevent people from engaging in dangerous sports, or requiring people to take safety precautions when they take part in dangerous activities. (There is a problem in applying this principle, because of vagueness in the phrase 'harm others'. It is quite difficult to think of harm to one person which would have no impact on others – for example serious injury to a mountaineer is likely to cause some suffering to her family).

3 Newspapers should be allowed to publish views which are insulting and offensive to particular groups or individuals.

4 Doctors should tell patients the truth about the seriousness of their illnesses, or about the risks involved in operations.

5 Suppose a friend has confessed to you that he was involved in a crime, and you have promised to tell no one. You then find out that someone else is likely to go to prison for this crime, and that, apart from your friend, you are the only person who knows that he is the culprit. This principle tells you that you should tell no one else the truth.

Exercise 18: Clarifying words or phrases

1 This argument concludes that in order to be beautiful, you only have to be *average*, rather than being unusual. The evidence for this claim comes from an experiment in which pictures of faces which had been made up of parts of a number of individual faces were generally judged to be more attractive than any genuine individual face.

The word which needs clarification here is 'average'. The composite faces in the experiment could be said to be average in the sense of being a sum of little bits of different people's faces (e.g. the length of a nose might have been determined by adding up the lengths of 16 different noses and dividing by sixteen). But the conclusion contrasts being average with being unusual, which suggests that here 'average' is being taken to mean 'typical'. Someone whose face has the 'average' dimensions of the composite faces in the experiment may not be 'average' in the sense of being typical. Such a person may be very unusual.

2 This passage concludes that *empathy* is a necessary but not a sufficient characteristic for being a good citizen. The example used to show that empathy is necessary in order to be a good citizen is of people who lack empathy in the sense of lacking concern about the suffering of others.

But the example used to show that empathy is insufficient for being a good citizen (the businessman who understands the feelings of others, and uses this understanding to exploit them) appears to define empathy as 'understanding the feelings of others', rather than 'caring about the suffering of others'. If empathy means merely understanding the feelings of others, then empathy is not sufficient for being a good citizen. But if empathy means both understanding and caring about the feelings and sufferings of others, then empathy is a good basis for being a good citizen.

3 This passage recommends that doctors should be *honest* with their patients, for two reasons:

- telling lies can lead to a breakdown of trust, and
- patients have a right to know everything about their medical condition.

This second reason is also used to support the claim that those patients who ask about their condition should be given truthful answers to their questions. This could be taken to suggest both that patients who do not ask about their condition do not need to be told, and that those who do ask do not need to be given more information than is included in truthful answers to their direct questions.

But 'being honest' could be construed not just as 'not telling lies', but as 'giving all the information one has'. The second reason – that patients have a right to know everything about their medical condition – seems to support this second interpretation of 'being honest'. If doctors are to be told to 'be honest' with their patients, it has to be clear whether this means simply 'never tell lies to patients' or 'give full information to patients, whether they ask or not'.

Exercise 19: Writing a summary

In each of these answers a brief summary is given with which your summary can be compared. However, your summary can be a good one even if it does not exactly match the example, since you were asked to express the summary in your own words.

1 This passage is trying to convince me of two things. First, fox hunting is an unpleasant (repellent) activity, on the grounds that:

- it involves killing for pleasure;
- tradition is no defence of it; and

- compassion about animals is a measure of a society becoming more civilised.

Second, despite being repellent, fox hunting should not be banned, on the grounds that:

- the state should not intervene where harm to others is not over-whelming; and
- the cruelty case against foxes is not clear cut.

Support is offered for the claim that tradition is no defence by mentioning other 'traditional' activities – badger baiting and cockfighting – which are now illegal.

Support is offered for the claim that the cruelty case is not clear cut in the statements that, despite their 'fluffy' image, foxes are predators which have been controlled for centuries, and that the anti-hunting lobby hasn't made a convincing case that other methods of slaughter are less cruel. This part of the argument relies on the assumption that it is necessary for farmers and landowners to continue to control fox numbers.

2 This passage is trying to convince me that the Government should require employers to give a fortnight's paid paternity leave to fathers, on the grounds that this would be good for families and could be good for business.

The claim that it would be good for families is supported by the following reasons:

- fathers are a key support, because mothers have to leave maternity wards as soon as possible, and many lack extended families to back them up;
- post natal depression is less prevalent when the father is actively involved;
- breast-feeding is more successful when dads are more supportive and well-informed;
- fathers can learn something about child care from health visitors during the first fortnight of their baby's life;
- more and more children are in sole care of their fathers more of the time;
- ignorant fathers are a danger to their children.

The claim that it can be good (or at least not bad) for business is supported by the following claims:

- it would do no harm (to business) to allow fathers get to know their babies for two weeks before returning to the treadmill, because new dads in Britain increase their hours of work, and work the longest hours in Europe; and
- Australia's largest insurer has found that giving new dads six weeks' paid paternity leave saves them money through reduced staff turnover.

3   This passage is trying to convince me that people should be allowed to sell one of their kidneys to someone who needs a transplant, on the grounds that:

- organs for transplantation are in very short supply;
- transplants of donated organs negate the idea that our bodies are sacred and nothing should be taken from them;
- people should be allowed to do what they like with their own bodies;
- selling a kidney for money does not harm anyone else;
- poor people will be able to get some money from the sale of a kidney; and
- the practice of selling kidneys could be regulated to prevent abuse, in a manner analogous to the control there is over the way we sell our labour.

The claim that people should be able to do what they like with their own bodies is offered some support by the suggestion that patients have rights over their own bodies, and that in the medical sphere there is an emphasis on patient autonomy. In addition, other examples are presented of ways in which people are allowed to take risks with their own bodies.

Exercise 20: Ten longer passages to evaluate

For this exercise, answers are provided for only three passages – numbers 1, 6 and 9. Each answer gives one possible analysis of the passage – your analysis may differ and yet be a good analysis. Your evaluation of the passage may also differ, because some of these issues are topical, and when you do your evaluation, you may be aware of new evidence which has come to light.

Passage 1: Cry-babies and colic

1   *Conclusion and reasons*: The passage is trying to get us to accept that the incessant crying of some babies during the first three months of life is

not due to 'colic', but is due to distress caused by nervousness and anxiety in the mother. The reasons given for this are:

- 'colic' crying ceases, as if by magic, around the third or fourth month of life ... at just the point where the baby is beginning to be able to identify its mother as a known individual;
- mothers with cry-babies are tentative, nervous and anxious in their dealings with their offspring, whereas mothers with quieter infants are deliberate, calm and serene; and
- babies are acutely aware of differences in tactile 'security' and 'safety', on the one hand, and tactile 'insecurity' and 'alarm' on the other.

2 *Assumptions*: There are two assumptions relating to explanations. The assumption which must be added to the first reason above is that the correct explanation of the baby's ceasing to cry at three months is that a bond has been formed with the mother. The assumption which must be added to the second reason above is that the correct explanation of the connection between babies' crying on the one hand and mothers' nervousness and anxiety on the other is that the anxiety of the mother causes the baby to cry.

3 *Assessing reasons/assumptions*: Is it true that so-called 'colic' crying ceases at three months? Many mothers with 'cry-babies' would confirm this. Is it true that three months is the age at which babies form a bond with the mother? Since the baby cannot be asked about its feelings, we have to judge this from the baby's behaviour. Psychologists observe behaviour such as eye contact, smiling at a familiar face, distress when a familiar person goes away. Many psychologists accept that the process of forming attachments to mothers is gradual, but there is some evidence of it as early as three months.

Is it true that mothers with babies who cry a lot are anxious, whereas those with quieter babies are calm? Although the passage does not explicitly say that observations of a sample of mothers have been done, it seems to suggest that this is so. If such studies have not been done, they could be done, and provided a large and representative sample of mothers were chosen, they could provide strong evidence for or against this claim.

Is it true that babies are aware of differences in tactile 'security' and 'safety', on the one hand, and tactile 'insecurity' and 'alarm' on the other? Again, this can only be concluded from observation of their behaviour, and in order to evaluate the truth of the claim, we should look at any evidence which psychologists have produced. Both the assumptions we identified were to do with explanations, so we will consider their plausibility under 6 below.

4 *Authorities cited*: The passage does not refer to any authorities, but in order to evaluate the truth of the reasons, we would perhaps have to rely on the authority of psychologists who had observed the behaviour of babies.

5 *Further evidence*: Did you think of any additional information which would strengthen or weaken the conclusion?

6 *Explanations*: We identified two explanations. The first was that the cessation of the baby's crying at three months is due to the formation of a bond between mother and infant. Even if we found good evidence of the formation of such a bond, it would not follow that the bond caused the cessation of crying. Another possible explanation for the cessation of crying is that some young babies do indeed have a physical problem, and that they cry because they are in pain. This is what is usually assumed by those who refer to the problem as 'colic'. They assume that the digestive system of some very young babies may produce a great deal of wind which can cause pain, but that such problems disappear as the baby grows.

The second explanation was of the fact that mothers with cry-babies are tentative, nervous and anxious in their dealings with their offspring, whereas mothers with quieter infants are deliberate, calm and serene. The explanation taken for granted was that the mother's anxiety caused the baby's crying. Another possible explanation is that the baby's crying causes the mother's anxiety. Perhaps one way to test which explanation is correct would be to take a sample of babies who were assumed to have 'colic', and to see if they cried less when looked after by someone who was calm and serene. One could in principle get additional evidence by taking a sample of quiet babies and seeing if their crying increased when they were looked after by someone who was anxious and nervous, but perhaps it would be ethically less acceptable to do this.

7 *Comparisons*: No comparisons are made in the passage.

8 *Further conclusions*: No firm conclusions can be drawn from the passage.

9 *Parallel reasoning*: Perhaps you noticed that the reasoning relied on the assumption that because X and Y occur together, X causes Y. You can probably think of an example which shows that this conclusion does not necessarily follow.

10 *General principles*: The passage does not use any general principles.

11 *Do the reasons support the conclusion?*: The chief weakness of the reasoning is that no evidence is offered as to why the explanations upon which the conclusion relies are the correct explanations. Perhaps the author knows that there is good evidence for such a view, but it is not presented in this passage.

Passage 6: We should recycle the dead to help the living

1 *Conclusion and reasons*: This article aims to convince us that 'all organs from dead bodies should be automatically available at death without any consent being required', on the grounds that such a scheme will save lives, and that, although there will be significant costs, these 'are not incompatible with the values of a decent society'.

The reasons are identified in more detail below.

(a) There is a crisis in organ donation.

(b) The donor card scheme is failing us all.

(c) Both potential donors (and their relatives) and potential recipients (and their families) are entitled to our concern.

(d) We have not shown the same consideration to these two groups.

(e) Making organs available without consent being required would express an equality of concern for these two groups.

(f) The dead have no further use for their organs; the living do.

(g) The proposal (to dispense with the need for consent) would have many advantages.

(h) It seems doubtful that there would be many religious objections.

(i) Prudential self-interest supports the automatic availability of cadaver organs.

(j) It is almost certain that we can accommodate 'conscience based objections', and still save the lives of all those who are dying for want of donor organs.

Reasons (a) and (b) are given support by figures (5,000 needing kidney transplants, fewer than half the number of registered donors to meet the demand, 30 per cent of relatives refusing consent) aiming to show that many hundreds of people are dying every year in the UK for want of donor organs.

Reason (d) is offered support by the statement that as a society we have leant over backwards to make sure that potential donors and their relatives are protected against anything that might cause them distress or unease. Presumably this refers to the practices of asking for the consent of relatives to use the organs even of those who carry donor cards, and of not using these organs without such consent.

Support is offered for reason (e) by contrasting what each group stands to lose if their preferences are not respected. The potential recipients will lose their lives. The potential donors who are unwilling to donate will know that one of their wishes will not be respected.

The advantages cited in support of reason (g) are that more organs would be available, and that doctors would not have to ask dying people or grieving relatives for consent.

Reason (h) is supported by comparing a non-consensual scheme for organ donation with coroner ordered post-mortems, which cannot be vetoed by relatives of the dead person. The suggestion is that in both cases there is a strong public interest in not having to seek consent and not allowing anyone to opt out. It is claimed that since there has never been an outcry against compulsory post-mortems, it is unlikely that there would be an outcry against compulsory organ donation.

To support reason (i) the author presents two reasons why people need not be afraid that doctors will not strive to keep them alive if their organs are wanted. They are:

- there is no evidence that donor card carriers have not been given the best possible care; and
- each of us is more likely to need an organ and not get it than to be ill and not properly treated.

Support is presented for reason (j) by suggesting that a scheme of conscientious objection to organ donation, similar to schemes for conscientious objection to military service, would be feasible.

2 *Assumptions*: There is an assumption associated with reasons (c) and (d) that showing equal consideration to potential donors and potential recipients requires us to take measures to save the lives of potential recipients even if that means overruling the wishes of potential donors.

Associated with reason (g) is an assumption that it would be a good thing if doctors did not have to ask dying people or grieving relatives for consent to use organs – though it is not clear whether this is thought to be good from the doctors' point of view or from that of patients and relatives.

3 *Assessing reasons/assumptions*: There is no reason to doubt the claims associated with reasons (a) and (b) – i.e. the figures quoted, and in particular the claim that many people die who could be saved by transplants if more organs were available. The figures could in principle be checked.

Reason (c) is undeniably true – that both potential donors and potential recipients are entitled to our concern – but reason (d) is disputable. Who has not shown the same consideration to the two groups, and what would have to be done in order to show the same consideration? The author does not mean that medical staff do not show the same consideration to those in need of transplants – nurses and doctors can treat potential recipients of organs with consideration even if a transplant is not possible. The author means that 'society' has not shown the same consideration in that potential donors are allowed the choice as to whether to donate, and relatives are allowed to veto donation. Reason (e) provides the author's answer to what would show the same consideration – making organs available without having to get consent. The assumption associated with reasons (c), (d) and (e) – that, in relation to organ donation, the duty to save lives is more important than the requirement to get consent, is open to dispute. Clearly those in the medical profession have both duties, but the question as to which should take precedence where the two duties are in conflict is contentious.

Reason (f) is clearly true, if we interpret 'having a use for an organ' as meaning 'being able to benefit physically from the functioning of the organ'.

In relation to reason (g), it is almost certainly true that the proposed policy would result in the availability of more organs for transplant. The other supposed advantage is more debatable. It probably would be better for doctors if they did not have to ask difficult questions to dying people or grieving relatives. But would it be better for the general population? This would depend upon whether people think it is preferable to have no choice as to whether to donate their organs, or to be asked difficult questions at a distressing time.

The truth of reason (h) – that it is doubtful that there would be many religious objections – is questionable. This will be discussed in more detail under 'Further evidence' and 'Comparisons' below.

We identified two claims supporting reason (i). There is no reason to question the first of these, which suggests that donor card carriers receive the same care as anyone else, if ill or injured. If this implies that everyone who is ill or injured is 'properly treated', then the other claim is true also – i.e. that each of us is more likely to need an organ and not get it than to be ill and not properly treated. However, it should be noted that some people may have very little risk of needing a transplant, so it is not obvious that for each one of us 'prudential self-interest . . . supports the automatic availability of cadaver organs'.

The truth of reason (j) depends on the meaning of 'conscience based objections'. The author refers to them arising from religious belief or cultural practice. Perhaps it is true that there would be sufficiently few of these to be able to exempt such people and still have enough organs to meet demand. He does not specify exactly what criteria someone would have to satisfy in order to be exempted, and perhaps it would be difficult in practice to distinguish between those who have conscience based objections, and those who just don't like the idea of their organs being used.

4 *Authorities cited*: No authorities are mentioned in the article. The source of the figures quoted in the first paragraph is not given, but there is no reason to think the author would mislead us about these.

5 *Further evidence*: Three important points can be made in relation to further evidence on this topic.

- As long ago as 1999 when this article was written, there had been publicity about objections by parents to the organs of their dead children being used for medical research. More recently there has been outrage about the news that Alder Hey Hospital retained thousand of organs and body parts from deceased children, without seeking their parents' consent. It has been reported that subsequently fewer organs have been available for transplant, presumably because relatives will not give consent. This suggests that there may be massive opposition to the kind of scheme proposed by John Harris.
- 'Scandals' such as Alder Hey raise questions about ownership of body parts. One could simply say that of course deceased persons do not own their organs after death, because only living beings can be owners of anything. And yet we do recognise people's right to have their property disposed of as they would like when they die – why should kidneys differ from monetary wealth, which could prolong someone's life by paying for dialysis machines and health care? Moreover, we recognise the right of individuals to say in advance how they would like their remains to be disposed of – by burial or cremation; and of relatives to determine such matters on behalf of the deceased. Many parents of children who died in Alder Hey Hospital were greatly distressed by the thought that they had buried their child 'incomplete', and that the child had not been properly laid to rest. This suggests that a major shift in attitudes may be needed in order for Harris's proposal to gain general acceptance.
- If the aim of the proposed scheme is to increase the supply of organs in order to meet the demand for transplants, we could consider how other countries solve this problem. The article by Lewis Wolpert in Exercise 19 (p. 98) tells us that Spain and Austria have a scheme whereby individuals opt out of being a donor, rather than opting in –

i.e. if you object to being a donor, you carry a card to say so, otherwise it is assumed that you consent. He also claims that this means more organs are available for transplant than in Britain. Harris does not consider this possibility, but perhaps it could deal with the shortfall without too much public opposition.

6   *Explanations*: No explanations are offered in the passage.

7   *Comparisons*: The comparison is made between compulsory coroner ordered post-mortems and compulsory organ donation. The claim is that in both cases there is a clear and important public interest at stake, and we are invited to conclude that they will be alike also in that there would be few objections to compulsory organ donation.

It is probable that this comparison is made partly in order to convince us that we *shouldn't* object to compulsory organ donation, but also it is used as evidence that there *wouldn't* be much objection. We have already suggested that there is further evidence which casts doubt on this. Perhaps attitudes to the two practices differ because fewer people are affected by coroner ordered post-mortems than would be affected by compulsory organ donation, and perhaps many people do not see that the public interest is equal in both cases.

8   *Further conclusions*: No obvious firm conclusions can be drawn, though it is possible that there could be a better solution to the problem, as discussed under point 11 below. See also the comments in section 10 below about the implications of principles.

9   *Parallel reasoning*: No parallel arguments come to mind, but you may have thought of some.

10   *General principles*: Underlying the argument is the principle of 'equality of concern', and this is clearly an important principle. We should be equally concerned about the welfare of those whose illness could be cured by an organ transplant, and those who are ill or dying and do not want to donate their organs. The difficulty in applying this principle occurs when giving one group what they want requires denying the other group what they want. This difficulty could be expressed as a conflict between two further principles – that we should always do everything possible to save (or prolong) life, and that we should always respect people's choices about what happens to their own bodies. It is clear that Harris thinks that in relation to organ transplantation, the former principle overrides the latter. What is not clear is whether the principle that we should always do everything possible to

save (or prolong) life is meant to be an overriding principle with general application. If so, this could mean, for example, that governments should take the wealth of individuals and use it to save lives in poorer countries. Such issues take us into difficult philosophical and ethical territory, and they are discussed in more detail in my book, *Critical Reasoning in Ethics – a Practical Introduction*.

11   *Do the reasons support the conclusion?*: In relation to arguments which recommend a policy, we must consider:

- would the recommended policy or action be likely to achieve the desired aim?;
- would it have some undesirable effects?; and
- are there other, possibly better, ways of achieving the aim?

Let us assume that the aim of the policy is to ensure that the supply of organs meets the demand for transplants, or at least to save more lives of those in need of transplants. Yes, the policy would be likely to save more lives, and Harris did not have to produce much controversial reasoning to support this. The policy would probably meet the demand for transplants, if the criteria for conscience based objections were stringent.

Would there be undesirable consequences? There would be likely to be much more opposition to the introduction of such a policy than Harris envisages, and, judging from the reactions of parents in the Alder Hey 'scandal', a certain amount of distress on the part of relatives. There may be difficulties in determining the conditions for conscientious objection, and those denied exemption may feel that their rights were being infringed.

Could there be a better way of achieving the aim? It is, of course, possible that attitudes could change over time, and that most of us could come to accept that our bodies do not 'belong' to us, and that the state has the right to use parts of them for the benefit of others. But, given what appears to be resistance to this idea at present, a better solution may be to adopt the Spanish and Austrian schemes, which assume that everyone consents to the use of their organs after death, unless they carry a card forbidding this. If this scheme were tried, we could find out whether it would meet the demand for organs – and in the current climate of distrust, it may not. But perhaps it *would* provide enough organs, and if it did, this would surely be better than a compulsory scheme which upsets large numbers of people – even if we think their distress is not very logical.

We should refer back here to our initial summary of Harris's reasoning, which included the idea that, though there would be significant costs to his proposed scheme, these 'are not incompatible with the values of a decent society'. Although the author clearly wants to solve the problem of shortage in the supply of organs, his aim does not seem to be simply to solve this practical problem. He also wants to make ethical points about the values which any society should have. His comments suggest that a decent society would not allow us (except for a few conscientious objectors) to opt out of organ donation when people are dying for want of organs. However, a decent society should also take account of the concerns of all its citizens, and in particular people's concern that their wishes about the use of their bodies should be respected. If the practical problem could be solved by a scheme like those in Spain and Austria, which do not deny freedom of choice, then would this not be what a decent society should do?

Passage 9: Getting to the heart of the matter

1   *Conclusion and reasons*: The clue to the main conclusion is given in the introductory comment which heads the article – 'Drinking red wine will help you live longer? This is a fallacy'.

What exactly is meant by 'fallacy' here? Sometimes the word is used to mean 'false statement', and this interpretation would lead us to summarise the conclusion as – 'Drinking red wine will not help you live longer'.

However, the more precise meaning of 'fallacy' (used by logicians and critical thinkers) concerns the unsoundness of a process of reasoning. This interpretation would allow us to summarise the conclusion as – 'The idea that drinking red wine will help you live longer is based on unsound reasoning or evidence'. Note that this interpretation does not imply that the statement 'drinking red wine will help you live longer' is false – merely that the evidence or arguments presented for it do not establish that it is true.

The article clearly does rely on the second interpretation of 'fallacy' – in the first five paragraphs it sets out the argument usually presented to support the claim about red wine, and then attempts to show what is wrong with it. But perhaps the article also aims to show that it is probably untrue that drinking red wine will make you live longer, since it presents some possibly adverse consequences of red wine consumption.

Let us consider the reasoning in relation to the stronger claim – does it support a conclusion that – 'Drinking red wine will probably not make you live longer'?

There are three broad themes of reasoning aimed at supporting the following intermediate conclusions:

* red wine is only as good for you as beer [or white wine or spirits];
* drinking red wine is disadvantageous for some groups; and

- red wine has nothing to do with the low incidence of heart disease amongst the French.

(a) Red wine is only as good for you as beer [or white wine or spirits]
The reasoning towards the first of these intermediate conclusions is also intended to show that there is something wrong with the argument summarised in paragraphs 4 and 5 – in particular the assumption made by that argument that the association between red wine consumption and low heart disease rates in France is a causal one.

The reasons given in support of the intermediate conclusion are as follows.

To support the claim that white wine is as effective as red wine:

- This was first demonstrated in studies which compared those who drank only red wine with those who drank only white wine

The reasons to support the claim that beer and spirits are as effective as red wine:

- It seems that alcohol protects against heart disease by preventing the formation of blood clots.
- The thinning effects of alcohol on the blood are thought to last less than 24 hours.
- Beer and spirit drinkers are more likely to drink heavily once or twice a week, whereas wine drinkers may tend to spread out their consumption.

Supporting intermediate conclusions:

- Drinkers who take a small amount each day are more likely to benefit than those who take a lot at once.

and

- When [the differences in drinking patterns are] taken into account there is no difference in the relative benefits of drinking different tipples.

Some additional reasons to support the claim that the effects of red wine are no different from the effects of other alcoholic drinks:

- Little difference has been detected between blood samples in people who have imbibed the same amount of alcohol but in different forms.

- The positive effects of the alcohol itself – a shifted balance of cholesterol among the different constituents of the blood, and a reduced likelihood of blood aggregation – are common to all drinks.
- No one has yet found evidence that the fabled anti-oxidant phenolic compounds present in red wine actually increase in the bloodstream with the amount of red wine drunk.

(b) Drinking red wine is disadvantageous for some groups
The reasons offered for the second intermediate conclusion are as follows.

Reasons relating to Africa:

- for every man who dies there from heart disease, two will die a violent death;
- and in this situation, it seems that red wine consumption will not stop you being murdered.

Offered in support of an intermediate conclusion:

alcohol (including red wine) is not so good in sub-Saharan Africa.

Reasons relating to women:

- women have a lower risk of heart disease to start with;
- also ... the risks of drinking increase faster for women than they do for men. For instance, women have a greater susceptibility to liver damage; and the risk of breast cancer in women increases by about 10 per cent for each additional drink per day.

Offered in support of an intermediate conclusion:

- alcohol (once again, including red wine) is not so beneficial for women as it is for men.

Reasons relating to French men:

- The rate of death from heart disease in the UK may be three times that of France;
- but the rate of deaths from alcohol-related causes (including cancer of the mouth, cirrhosis of the liver and alcohol-related motor vehicle accidents) is three times higher in France than it is in the UK.

Offered in support of an intermediate conclusion:

- alcohol (still including red wine) is not necessarily beneficial for French men either.

Some additional reasons relating to effects of alcohol consumption:

- (And, incidentally, in the UK, where alcohol consumption is rising, the death rate from cirrhosis of the liver is also increasing.)
- (And anyone who is younger than their mid-40s, and therefore at low risk of heart disease will probably not benefit from alcohol at all – at least in this sense.)

(c) Red wine has nothing to do with the relatively low incidence of heart disease amongst the French
This intermediate conclusion is supported by a short argument and an alternative explanation for the low incidence of heart disease amongst the French.
    The argument is as follows.

Reasons:

- In France, the greater alcohol consumption is caused by more drinks per drinker rather than more drinkers.
- And all alcohol products protect against heart disease, but maximally at one to two units per day.

Conclusion:

- So the greater alcohol consumption of the French is not giving them any extra protection.

The alternative explanation for the low incidence of heart disease amongst the French – offered by two epidemiologists – is that until relatively recently the French diet has not been high enough in fat and cholesterol to produce as high a rate of heart disease at present as that in Britain.

2   *Assumptions*: The following assumptions can be identified:

- The studies comparing the effects of red wine consumption and white wine consumption are reliable.
- If red wine were more effective than other alcoholic drinks in protecting against heart disease, blood samples of those who had drunk red wine would differ from the samples of those who had imbibed other alcoholic drinks.

- It is unlikely that anti-oxidant phenolic compounds enter the blood-stream as a result of drinking red wine.
- Drinking alcohol before the mid-40s cannot confer any protection against heart disease in later life.
- The explanation given by the two epidemiologists of the low rate of heart disease amongst the French is the correct one.

3 *Assessing reasons/assumptions*: For the most part the truth of the reasons and assumptions cannot be assessed without either scientific knowledge or confirmation of statistics. There are claims about the effects of alcohol on the blood – information which derives from scientific evidence. And there are claims relating to statistics which could in principle be checked – for example, patterns of consumption of different forms of alcohol, rates of deaths from various causes, levels of risk of suffering from various diseases. There is also a claim about changes in the French diet.

4 *Authorities cited*: No authorities are mentioned in relation to the studies of the effects of alcohol. If we wish to judge the accuracy of the scientific evidence, we would have to find out who had carried out the various studies and consider whether they had any vested interest in making people believe that drinking specific forms of alcohol would reduce the risk of heart disease. For example a scientist paid by red wine producers could be said to have more of a vested interest than a scientist financed by the health service. Remember also the importance or corroboration – that if the same results are reported by a number of different studies, the more confident we can be about the accuracy of their claims.

Two scientists are mentioned in relation to the explanation of the French incidence of heart disease – Malcolm Law and Nicholas Wald, epidemiologists at the Wolfson Institute of Preventive Medicine at St Bartholomew's Hospital in London. There is no reason to doubt their expertise, since they are epidemiologists (specialists in patterns of disease); there is no reason to think they have a vested interest, given that they work for an institute which aims to find out the truth about causes of disease; and there is no reason to think that their research was not carried out properly, since their paper was published in a respectable journal (the *British Medical Journal*) and would have been peer reviewed (that is, critically assessed by other scientists).

Note, however, that their explanation is a *possible* explanation – we still need to assess it, which we shall consider under heading 6 below.

5 *Further evidence*: Further evidence could be sought in relation to the possible explanations of the differing rates of heart disease. If you have not

already come up with suggestions, think about it now, before you read the next section.

6 *Explanations*: There are explanations of three different facts:

- the difference in rates of heart disease between wine drinkers and those who drink beer or spirits;
- the fact that women benefit less than men from drinking alcohol; and
- the lower incidence of heart disease amongst the French.

Although not explicitly stated it is implied that wine drinkers have lower rates of heart disease than beer drinkers or spirit drinkers. The explanation is that this is due to different patterns of drinking. If it is true that beer and spirit drinkers drink less often, and that the beneficial changes to the blood from alcohol consumption last for only 24 hours, then this is a reasonable explanation.

It is not absolutely clear what is meant by – 'alcohol (once again, including red wine) is not so beneficial for women as it is for men'- but the explanations offered suggest two ways in which it may be less beneficial. The comment that women have a lower risk of heart disease than men suggests that what is being explained is that female alcohol drinkers do not reduce their risk of heart disease to the same extent as male alcohol drinkers. No evidence (such as statistics of susceptibility to heart disease for both men and women, and both drinkers and non-drinkers) is given to show that this is so, and it is not clear that this could be explained by women having a lower risk in the first place. Even if it were a good explanation, it would not show that it is not beneficial for women to drink alcohol, since that will reduce their risk to some extent.

The other explanation for women benefiting less than men is that the risks of drinking – in the sense of increased susceptibility to other diseases – increase faster for women than they do for men. This suggests that the fact which is being explained is that women who drink alcohol do not increase their chance of living longer to the same extent as do men who drink alcohol. Again, no evidence (in this case of statistics on average life-spans of male and female drinkers and non-drinkers) is given for this. If it were true, then it could be explained by increased susceptibility for women to liver damage and breast cancer.

The explanation for the lower incidence of heart disease amongst the French is a major theme of the article. The explanation in terms of the beneficial effects of drinking red wine is rejected, and some good reasoning is given for this, assuming that the following claims are true:

- In France, the greater alcohol consumption is caused by more drinks per drinker rather than more drinkers.
- And all alcohol products protect against heart disease, but maximally at one to two units per day

If the percentage of the population who consume alcohol is the same in the two countries, and if only two drinks per day are needed (regardless of whether one is French or British) in order to gain maximum protection against heart disease, then it cannot be the greater consumption of alcohol in France which accounts for the difference in rates of heart disease (although it could be different patterns of drinking between wine and beer drinkers – as the author would concede).

The alternative explanation offered in the article is plausible – that past differences in diet account for the difference in heart disease rates, especially since diet is known to have an effect on susceptibility to heart disease. If this is the correct explanation, and if it is true that fat or cholesterol consumption is now similar in the two countries, we would expect to see the rates of heart disease rising in France in future years. If this happens, it will help to confirm this explanation. If it does not, other possible explanations will need to be sought – for example, genetic differences between the two populations, differences in exercise habits, or other differences in diet – perhaps consumption by the French of foods which compensate for the increasing fat consumption.

7 *Comparisons*: The article discusses comparisons between different countries (France, Britain and the USA), between men and women, and between different alcoholic drinks. However, for the most part, it does not rely on simple unexamined analogies to support its conclusions.

For example, it challenges the idea that because the French consume a lot of red wine and have a low rate of heart disease, the British would lower their rate of heart disease if they consumed more red wine.

It does accept that red wine, white wine, beer and spirits are comparable in their effects on the heart. This is based on accepting the results of scientific studies, and the appropriateness of the comparison needs to be assessed by considering the reliability of the source of evidence.

There is an implicit comparison which could be challenged. The point of mentioning the adverse effects of alcohol on French men is to get us to accept that alcohol is not necessarily beneficial for men in general – hence we are being invited to accept that French men who drink alcohol and British men who drink alcohol are comparable in important respects. But the way in which they would have to be comparable in order to conclude that red wine would not be beneficial for British men is that they would have to consume similar amounts. However, we are told near the end of the passage that in France the greater alcohol consumption is caused by more drinks per drinker. So it is possible that British men could drink enough red wine to benefit the heart without risking cancer of the mouth and cirrhosis of the liver.

8 *Further conclusions*: The last sentence in section 7 above identifies a conclusion which the author could have drawn from his own comments, and which is at odds with one of the author's themes.

9 *Parallel reasoning*: No obvious parallel arguments come to mind.

10 *General principles*: The argument does not rely on any general principles.

11 *Do the reasons support the conclusion?*: We shall consider each of the three main themes which we have identified.

(a) Red wine is only as good for you as beer [or white wine or spirits]
The evidence from studies which compare the effects of red wine with the effects of other alcoholic drinks gives strong support (assuming that the studies are reliable) to a conclusion that drinking red wine is no more effective than certain other alcoholic drinks at reducing the risk of heart disease. However, it does not support the main conclusion, since it does not show that drinking red wine will not make you live longer than if you consumed no alcohol.

(b) Drinking red wine is disadvantageous for some groups
The comments about deaths in sub-Saharan Africa do nothing to support either the intermediate or the main conclusion, but perhaps the author does not offer them as serious reasons. The fact that red wine does not make murder victims live longer cannot support the claim that drinking red wine will not make some people live longer by making them less susceptible to heart disease. The appropriate way to interpret the conclusion – 'Drinking red wine will probably not make you live longer' – is as meaning – 'Drinking red wine will not increase anyone's chance of living longer', and not as meaning – 'Drinking red wine will not prevent early death'.

The evidence concerning the effects of alcohol on women's health could only support a conclusion that for *women* drinking red wine may not result in a longer life. However, the evidence quoted is insufficient even to support this limited conclusion, because we are not given information about the level of intake of alcohol which is likely to lead to liver damage and breast cancer.

It is possible that women could avoid liver damage and breast cancer, and at the same time gain some protection against heart disease, if they drank small amounts of red wine each day.

The comments about French men are presumably intended to make us accept that alcohol is not necessarily beneficial for men in general. However, the same criticism can be made as is made above in relation to the claims about women. We are not told what level of alcohol intake is required in order to suffer the adverse effects on health, but we are told that the French consume more drinks per drinker. It is possible that men could drink enough red wine to gain the benefits without being at risk of cancer of the mouth and cirrhosis of the liver. The comment about deaths in motor vehicle accidents is irrelevant – those who die in motor vehicle accidents caused by drink driving may not themselves be the drinkers, or the drivers, and those who drink a small amount of red wine each day are not necessarily going to drive whilst drunk.

(c) Red wine has nothing to do with the relatively low incidence of heart disease amongst the French

This section of the reasoning depends partly upon the plausibility of the explanation offered by the two epidemiologists. Their explanation is not implausible, but more evidence will be needed to confirm it.

It depends also on the claim that the greater consumption of red wine in France is caused by more drinks per drinker, which, if true, gives strong support to the intermediate conclusion.

However, the intermediate conclusion itself does not give strong support to a main conclusion that – 'Drinking red wine will probably not make you live longer', because even if the difference in red wine consumption is not the correct explanation of the lower incidence of heart disease amongst the French, nevertheless red wine could confer some protection. Indeed the author concedes that it does confer protection – to the same extent as other alcoholic drinks.

Bibliography and further reading

Copi, I. M. and Burgess-Jackson, K. (1992) *Informal Logic*, 2nd edn, New York: Macmillan.

Dewey, J. (1909) *How We Think*, London: D. C. Heath & Co.

Ennis, R. H. (1995) *Critical Thinking*, Englewood Cliffs, New Jersey: Prentice Hall.

Fisher, A. E. (1988) *The Logic of Real Arguments*, Cambridge: Cambridge University Press.

Freeman, J. B. (1988) *Thinking Logically*, Englewood Cliffs, New Jersey: Prentice Hall.

Glaser, E. (1941) *An Experiment in the Development of Critical Thinking*, New York: Teachers College, Columbia University.

Govier, T. (1985) *A Practical Study of Argument*, Belmont, California: Wadsworth Publishing Company.

Norris, S. P. and Ennis, R. H. (1989) *Evaluating Critical Thinking*, Pacific Grove, California: Midwest Publications.

Paul, R. (1990) *Critical Thinking*, Rohnert Park, California: Center for Critical Thinking and Moral Critique, Sonoma State University.

Phelan, P. and Reynolds, P. (1996) *Argument and Evidence: Critical Analysis for the Social Sciences*, London: Routledge.

Scriven, M. (1976) *Reasoning*, New York: McGraw Hill.

Scriven, M. and Fisher, A. E. (1996) *Critical Thinking: Defining and Assessing It*, Point Reyes, California: Edge Press.

Siegel, H. (1988) *Educating Reason*, London and New York: Routledge.

Swartz, R. and Parks, S. (1992) *Infusing Critical and Creative Thinking into Content Instruction*, Pacific Grove, California: Critical Thinking Press and Software.

Thomson, A. (1999) *Critical Reasoning in Ethics – a Practical Introduction*, London and New York, Routledge.

Warburton, N. (2000) *Thinking from A to Z*, 2nd edn, London and New York: Routledge.

Weston, A. (1992) *A Rulebook for Arguments*, 2nd edn, Indianapolis and Cambridge: Hackett Publishing Company.

Index